The Sanctuary
of the Soul

C. T. Lewis

WESTBOW
PRESS
A DIVISION OF THOMAS NELSON

WestBow Press books may be ordered through booksellers or by contacting:

WestBow Press
A Division of Thomas Nelson
1663 Liberty Drive
Bloomington, IN 47403
www.westbowpress.com
1-(866) 928-1240

ISBN: 978-1-4497-8671-7 (sc)
ISBN: 978-1-4497-8672-4 (e)
ISBN: 978-1-4497-8670-0 (hc)

Library of Congress Control Number: 2013903352

Printed in the United States of America

WestBow Press rev. date: 03/08/2013

Table of Contents

PART I
THE DESTINY OF MAN

PART II
THE DESTINY OF MAN MADE POSSIBLE

PART III
THE DESTINY OF MAN MADE ACTUAL

For My Parents

A Note on the Translation

The New International Version (NIV) provides the default translation. In many instances, however, in order to reflect as clearly as possible the train of thought presented by the author, it has been necessary to translate from other versions (especially the JPS or NRSV), and in some cases directly from the biblical text itself.

Acknowledgments

The contents of this book arose out of numerous sermons, lectures, and talks conducted over the course of many years. It would not have been possible without the support of the congregation of Troy Christian Chapel, the missionaries of the King's Lodge in England, and the students, parents, and staff of Christian Leadership Academy. My heartfelt gratitude goes out to all of those who have sat under my teaching, and through whom I have learned so much.

INTRODUCTION

God is spirit, and his worshippers must
worship him in spirit and in truth.

John 4:24

I

To "worship in spirit" is to worship at the sanctuary within one's own soul. The scriptures provide us with a pattern for how this is to be done in the ancient system of temple worship established under Moses. Jesus Christ is the supreme exemplar and the supreme executor of that pattern: he is the incarnation of the temple, and his work consists in transforming his disciples into temples like himself. Through the gift of his blood, he renders their souls fit to serve as dwelling places for the deity; and through the gift of his body, he fills their souls with the presence of God.

This briefly summarizes the governing idea behind the present book, the remainder of which consists in unpacking its meaning in greater depth and in rendering it applicable to the life of the Christian. Perhaps the greatest obstacle to this task is that few modern believers take an interest in the ancient practices of temple worship. If it were true that these practices amounted to nothing more than a collection of obsolete laws and rituals, this lack of interest would be justified. But it is one of the aims of this book to show that these matters are not only relevant but have been preserved precisely in order to furnish us with a roadmap for the governance of our inner lives. Even though the believer may not observe these laws and rituals outwardly, they are nevertheless intended to understand, practice, and experience them inwardly.

To put the matter differently, I should like to re-establish the Torah as the spiritual center of the Old and New Testaments. Although Christians have sometimes been inclined to talk as though there were a fundamental discontinuity between the old and the new, I will be advancing the idea that the old is taken up, preserved, and transformed in the new. Jesus' own teaching provides the most authoritative ground for this view, and the following passage has in many ways served as my inspiration for the whole book: *Do not think that I have come to abolish the Torah or the Prophets; I have not come to abolish them but to fulfill them. I tell you the truth, until heaven and earth disappear, not the smallest letter, not the least stroke of a pen, will by any means disappear from the Torah until everything is accomplished. Anyone who breaks one of the least of these commands and teaches others to do the same will be called least in the Kingdom of God, but whoever practices and teaches these commands will be called great in the Kingdom of God* (Matt. 5:17-19).

II

In the writing of this book, I have been guided primarily by the scriptures, as well as by the writings of a variety of theologians, philosophers, and scholars, and of course by such experiences as have emerged in the course of my own spiritual development. There is hardly a paragraph of this work that could not have been expanded into a whole chapter should I have wished to include an extensive account of my reasoning, or a survey of supporting and opposing views, or the thrust and counter-thrust of argument. Instead, I have chosen to present the vision of this book as simply as possible, devoting my attention to the economy, clarity, and distinction of its central thesis.

The book is divided into three parts, the titles of which exhibit the structure of the whole: (1) the Destiny of Man; (2) the Destiny of Man Made Possible; (3) and the Destiny of Man Made Actual. Each section lays the foundation for the one's that follow it, with the result that the first three chapters are almost exclusively devoted to theoretical matters. For some readers this may prove to be a breath of fresh air, while others may wish to begin with the second section of the book (as it deals with the more practical issue of redemption), and still others with the third section of the book (as it deals with the most practical issue of all, the application of redemption). In all of these chapters, however, I have avoided the popular convention of hiding tiny bits of theology within dramatic personal narratives, so that even the devotional sections contain a relatively dense concentration of ideas.

While my only direct quotations are from scripture, I nevertheless wish to acknowledge a few individuals whose writings have been especially influential in the development of my own thought. Among classical religious writers, I mention the perennially relevant works of Augustine and Aquinas, the mystics Teresa of Avila and John of the Cross, and the puritans John Owen and Jonathan Edwards. Among more modern writers, I have benefited greatly from the works of Rudolph Otto, Søren Kierkegaard, Maurice Blondel, G. K. Chesterton, C. S. Lewis, Dietrich Bonhoeffer, Karl Barth, A. W. Tozer, and Thomas Merton. A special debt of gratitude goes to Marc Brettler, who assisted me in the translation of a number of terms, and to the late Jacob Milgrom, whose scholarly work on the books of Exodus, Leviticus, and Numbers has proved a constant source of inspiration and insight.

I hope that the present work will find an audience among all who harbor within themselves a genuine hunger after the things of God. In an age dominated by secular interests, and in which much of the western church has fallen under the shadow of the businessman, the spiritual vision of this book will no doubt seem out of step with the demands of the times. Nevertheless, it has not been written in order to serve the needs of the many who stand on the broad path of life, but to serve the needs of the few who have made it their ambition to lead a quiet life in devotion to the spiritual growth of themselves, their families, and their church communities. It is above all to this end that I offer the following work, that we may reopen the wells dug by our forefathers, and that we may shine a light on the path that leads to infinite communion with God through Jesus Christ.

C. T. Lewis, 2013

The Sanctuary

MOST HOLY PLACE   HOLY PLACE   OUTER COURTYARD

N

PRESENCE   INCENSE   BREAD

W

THE LAVER
OF WATER

THE ALTAR
OF SACRIFICE

E

VEIL   LIGHT

S

PART I
THE DESTINY OF MAN

CHAPTER ONE

The Kingdom of God

*The time is fulfilled; the Kingdom of God has come
near; repent, and believe the good news.*

Mark 1:15

In Jesus' earthly ministry, the fundamental theme of his preaching is captured in the little phrase, "The Kingdom of God": *Now after John was arrested, Jesus came to Galilee, proclaiming the good news of God, and saying, "The time is fulfilled; the Kingdom of God has come near; repent, and believe the good news"* (Mk 1:14-15).

When Jesus spoke in this way, he was not introducing a new idea, but taking up an old idea, and one that already had a long currency in the history of Israel. If we would hear what he is trying to say to us, we must try to see it in the historical context he placed it in. If we would understand the New Testament, we must first understand the Old Testament.

In the book of Genesis, God is portrayed as the great king over creation, and man is presented as living in rebellion against him. The whole of the biblical narrative that follows can be viewed as a story about the deity's restoration of that kingdom. This he achieves through his covenant, a solemn contract in which he binds himself and his people to the terms of his sovereign rule. The spatial and temporal center out of which this covenant operates is the sanctuary, the deity's palace and the place from which his decrees, laws, and judgments go forth into all the earth. Now Jesus is the incarnation of that sanctuary: he fulfills the terms of the covenant, and he re-establishes the deity's governance on earth beginning with his own self. Through him, we too are called to belong to this kingdom, to enter into this covenant, and to become sanctuaries indwelt by the presence of the living God.

The Creational Kingdom of God

God's kingship achieves its first expression in his rule over the primeval sea. According to the scriptures, creation did not begin as an orderly whole, but as a chaotic, dead, and barren mass of earth submerged in dark waters: *In the beginning, God created the heavens and the earth. Now the earth was barren and empty, darkness was over the face of the deep, and the breath of God was moving over the face of the waters* (Gen. 1:1-2).

In the Bible, God brings forth of a kingdom of living creatures from this raw material, and the biblical poets dramatize this event as a battle between YHWH and Leviathan (a monster personifying the primeval sea). In this battle, God uses the breath of his mouth to subdue the sea monster, after which the divine breath and the tamed sea reappear as the fundamental elements of creaturely life. First, he fashions creatures from the dust of the earth and breathes into their nostrils the breath of life: *How many are the things you have made, O Lord: the earth is full of your creatures... When you take away their breath, they die and return to the dust. When you send back your breath, they are created* (Ps. 104:24 and 29-30). Second, he sustains the creatures he has made by channeling all of the sea's destructive torrents into fertile streams, making the earth productive of food, and its creatures productive of offspring: *O God, my king from old, who brings deliverance upon the earth: it was you who drove back the sea by your power, who broke the heads of the monster in the waters; it was you who crushed the heads of the Leviathan, who gave him as food to the creatures of the desert* (Ps. 74:12-14).

In this way, the Kingdom of God assumes its most basic form in creation. As a kingdom teeming with living things, this divine order is not expressed in the eternal unfolding of an abstract principle or in a deterministic chain of causes and effects, but in the free call of the Creator and the free response of his creatures. The Creator's call consists in the manifestation of his glory to his creatures: *The heavens declare the glory of God, the sky proclaims the work of his hands. Day after day they pour forth speech; night after night they display knowledge. There is no speech or language where their voice is not heard. Their voice goes out into all the earth, their words to the ends of the world* (Ps. 19:1-4). And the creatures' response consists in the giving of glory to his Creator: *All your works will praise you, O Lord; all your saints will bless you. They will tell of the glory of your kingdom, and speak of your might, so that all men may know of your mighty acts and the glorious splendor of your kingdom. Your kingdom is an eternal kingdom, and your dominion endures for all generations* (Ps. 145:10-13).

The Creation as a Sanctuary of God

Now if the Kingdom of God is expressed in the giving and receiving of glory, then the primary function of the created order can be none other than to serve this purpose. In other words, the created order may be regarded as a sanctuary: a place for housing the deity's presence, and for manifesting his character and calling forth divine worship: *I will see you in the sanctuary. I will behold your might and glory. Because your love is better than life, my lips will glorify you* (Ps. 63:2-3).

Furthermore, a careful reading of the creation story indicates that it is intended to be read as an account about the construction of a sanctuary. Above all, this is exhibited in the parallelism between the creation of the world and the construction of the Tabernacle, both of which are structured around seven divine commands, culminating in the Sabbath (cf. the seven days of creation with Ex. 25:1, 30:11, 30:17, 30:22, 30:34, 31:1, and 31:12): *God saw all that he had made, and behold: it was very good... So God blessed the seventh day* (Gen. 1:31 and 2:3); *Moses saw all their work, and behold: they did it just as YHWH had commanded. So Moses blessed them* (Ex. 39:43).

Again, since the most basic function of a sanctuary was to provide a resting place for the spirit of a deity, the function of creation may be said to consist in providing a resting place for the spirit of YHWH. Accordingly, the seventh day is not only a day on which the divinity rests from his work, but also a day on which the divinity rests within his work. On the day of rest, the created order is brought to completion not only because it has been created, but also because it has been indwelt by YHWH: *For YHWH has chosen Zion, he has desired it for his dwelling: "This is my resting place forever and ever; here I will sit enthroned, for I have desired it"* (Ps. 132:13-14). Therefore, in Isaiah, God declares: *Heaven is my throne, and the earth is my footstool. Where is the house you will build for me? Where will my resting place be?* (Is. 66:1).

The Creature as an Icon of God

In ancient times, after the construction of a temple, an image of the deity was installed inside the shrine of that temple. In the Bible this same pattern is evident: after the creation of the world, the human creature is installed within it, having been made "in the image and likeness of God" (Gen. 1:26).

This word "image" is a translation of the Hebrew word *tselem* and the Greek word *eikon*. Now while the function of a sanctuary is to house the presence of a deity, the function of an icon is to reflect the glory of that deity. Thus, the role of man is to dwell in the sanctuary of God, so that he might become a reflection of the glory of God. He fulfills this role by living in communion with God, whereby he reflects the divine glory into himself and whereby he reflects the divine glory back out into the world. Insofar as man reflects the divine glory into himself, he is a son of God: *God said, "Let us make man in our image, in our likeness* (Gen. 1:26a). Insofar as man reflects the divine glory back out into the world, he is a royal steward of God, ruling over the earth and its creatures: *And let them rule over the fish of the sea, and the birds of the air, over the livestock, over all the wild animals, and over all the creatures that move along the ground* (Gen. 1:26b).

As the divine presence rests within the sanctuary, so the soul of man finds its rest within the sanctuary. To dwell in the midst of the divine presence is to find rest: *My presence will go with you, and I will give you rest* (Ex. 33:14). To be removed from the divine presence is to be condemned to a restless existence: *I will be hidden from your presence and become a restless wanderer on the earth* (Gen. 4:14). Indeed, it is only here that the soul can find rest, for it is only here that the soul can fulfill is divinely appointed vocation to serve as the icon of God: *My soul finds rest in God alone; my deliverance comes from him. He alone is my rock and my deliverance; he is my fortress, I will never be shaken* (Ps. 62:1-2). Although man's divinely appointed vocation can easily become buried beneath a heap of temporal concerns, it nevertheless continues to announce its presence in the most profound longings of the human heart: *As the deer pants for streams of water, so my soul pants for you, O God. My soul thirsts for God, for the living God. O when will I come to appear before God!* (Ps. 42:1-2).

The Ruination of the Icon and the Sanctuary

The fall of man is essentially an account of the shattering of the deity's icon and the abandoning of the deity's sanctuary. According to the Bible, a mysterious being depicted as a serpent insinuated itself into man's thoughts, tempting him to reject the rule of God, and thereby introduced rebellion into the Kingdom of God.

Although the serpent is traditionally regarded as an evil spirit invading the world from the outside, the scriptures simply describe him as "the craftiest of all the creatures made by God" (Gen. 3:1). The most natural interpretation of this statement is that the serpent is a personification of the power of chaos that was subdued in the creation of the world. This interpretation is born out in biblical poetry, where the image of the serpent is clearly identified with the monster of the sea. This is the creature who was subdued at the beginning of creation: *By YHWH's power he churned up in the sea; by his wisdom he cut Rahab to pieces. By his breath the skies became fair; his hand pierced the gliding serpent* (Job 26:12-13). And this is also the creature who will be subdued once more at the end of time: *In that day, YHWH will punish with his sword, his fierce, great, and powerful sword, Leviathan the gliding serpent, Leviathan the coiling serpent; he will slay the monster of the sea* (Is. 27:1).

Having been enticed by the ancient power that lay at the heart of creation, mankind fell away from God. In his rebellion against God, he acquired a new independence for himself, but was by the very same token cast out from the sanctuary of God and his iconic status was reduced to a heap of broken images. Moreover, he himself became a portal through which the power of chaos was able to re-enter creation, rendering him unfit to serve as the icon of God, and rendering the world unfit to serve as the sanctuary of God. As a result, the material conditions of his life were placed under a curse: the earth becoming uncooperative in its production of food (Gen. 3:17), and the womb becoming uncooperative in its production of offspring (Gen. 3:16). Ultimately, the spiritual conditions of his life were withdrawn as well: his mortal body returning to the ground, and his life-breath returning to God (Gen. 3:19 and Eccl. 12:7). As God's kingship found its greatest expression in the creation of man and the world, so it found its greatest suppression in the ruin of man and the world. Although from the sovereign perspective of the deity, the created order remained in the providential security of his eternal rest, from the limited perspective of man, the quality of rest had now been replaced by a brooding restlessness. It is upon this basis that we now speak of the deity's covenant, for it is through his covenant that man retains the hope of re-entering that rest: *Thus, there remains a Sabbath-rest for the people of God, for anyone who enters his rest also rests from his own work. Therefore, let us make every effort to enter that rest* (Heb. 4:9-11).

The Covenantal Kingdom of God

The remainder of the biblical narrative is largely taken up with the story of the restoration of the Kingdom of God: that is, the reassertion of the deity's rule over the primeval sea through the redemption of man as his icon and the world as his sanctuary.

At this point, however, God's rule expresses itself not only in the natural world of creation, but also in the history of man. As the kingdom was broken through a historic act of man, so the kingdom is restored through the historic acts of the deity, which in turn become the legal precedents for the establishment of his divine law. This twofold response provides the basis for the ancient distinction between biblical narrative and biblical law, which reappears in the literature of the rabbis as *Aggadah* and *Halakhah*. Together, they constitute the deity's covenant or *Berit*: the deeds and the laws of his covenant are now the means whereby he restores his kingdom, the means whereby he re-creates man and the world, and the means whereby he brings all things into his rest.

As there is only one Kingdom of God, so there is really only one covenant whereby its governance is restored. Nevertheless, this one covenant progressively unfolds in several different stages, each of which builds upon the foundation of those previous to it. As we approach the first stage of this covenantal progression, we are confronted by the most fundamental problem posed by the fall, for the whole race stands opposed to the deity's purpose: namely, that of establishing a sanctuary for himself in which man might reflect the glory of God. Apart from this purpose, there is no real justification for the existence of man or the world:

I have decided to put an end to all flesh, for the earth is filled with lawlessness because of them. I am going to destroy both them and the earth (Gen. 6:13). If, therefore, there is to be a restoration of the Kingdom of God, then the covenant whereby it is restored must begin by establishing terms for the preservation of both man and the world: *I establish my covenant with you: Never again will all life be cut off by the waters of a flood; never again will there be a flood to destroy the earth* (Gen. 9:11). This carries with it the profound implication that the whole of reality exists for the sake of the covenant that redeems it, a view expressed in the Jewish teaching that all of reality exists for the sake of Israel and her Messiah, and in the Christian teaching that all of reality exists for the sake of Christ and his Church: *I will proclaim the decree of YHWH: He said to me, "You are my Son; today I have become your Father. Ask of me, and I will make the nations your inheritance, the ends of the earth your possession. You will rule them with an iron scepter; you will dash them to pieces like pottery. Therefore, you kings, be wise; be warned, you rulers of the earth. Serve YHWH with fear and rejoice with trembling. Kiss the Son, lest he be angry and you be destroyed in your way, for his wrath can flare up in a moment. Blessed are all who take refuge in him* (Ps. 2:7-12).

YHWH's Kingship over the Flood

In the creation story, YHWH brings order out of chaos. But in the fall story, man brings chaos out of order. Sin is, so to speak, the door through which the power of chaos re-enters the world, culminating in the corruption of man and the earth: *Now the earth became corrupt in God's sight and was full of lawlessness. God saw how corrupt the earth had become, for all the people on earth had corrupted their ways* (Gen. 6:12).

Although man did not intend it, the terms of his alliance with chaos made provision for the undoing of the whole created order: the withdrawal of the breath of life from its creatures, and the re-immersion of the earth in the sea. In other words, sin by its very nature invited upon itself the catastrophe we call "the flood." And thus, the flood should not be regarded as an arbitrary act of divine retribution, but rather as a granting of what man had implicitly agreed to in his ill-conceived pact with evil. Nevertheless, as YHWH's kingship first achieved expression in his rule over the sea, so it now achieves expression in his rule over the flood. He does not permit the flood to thwart his divine purpose, but he harnesses it, subdues it, and puts it to work as a servant of his own ends. Thus, the scripture says of Leviathan: *He looks down on all that are haughty; he is king over all that are proud* (Job 41:34). But it says of YHWH: *The Lord sits enthroned over the flood; The Lord is enthroned as king forever* (Ps. 29:10).

In this way, the will of man retains its freedom, and the will of the deity retains its sovereignty. Man's self-invoked destruction does not prevent the deity from manifesting his glory to creation, but simply provides an occasion for him to manifest it in a different way: namely, through the redemptive power of his justice and grace. God demonstrates his justice when he allows the waters of the flood to swallow up the sin of man and the world: *You covered [the earth] with the deep as with a garment; the waters stood above the mountains* (Ps. 104:6). But God demonstrates his grace when he saves a remnant of humanity in the ark, and when he checks the waters of the flood and once more channels them into life-giving streams: *But at your rebuke the waters fled, at the sound of your thunder they took to flight; they flowed over the mountains, they went down into the valleys, to the place you assigned for them. You set a boundary they cannot cross; never again will they cover the earth. He makes springs pour water into the ravines; it flows between the mountains. They give water to all the beasts of the field; the wild donkeys quench their thirst. The birds of the air nest by the waters; they sing among the branches. He waters the mountains from his upper chambers; the earth is satisfied by the fruit of his work. He makes grass grow for the cattle, and plants for man to cultivate—bringing forth food from the earth* (Ps. 104:7-14).

The Flood Narrative

Thus, the flood narrative begins with a reversal of creation: the breath of life is withdrawn from its creatures and the earth is re-immersed in the sea: *By God's word the heavens existed and the earth was formed out of water and by water. By these waters also the world of that time was deluged and destroyed* (II Pet. 3:5-6). Nevertheless, when we speak of the flood as a reversal of creation, we are not primarily concerned with its geographical extent. For, as we have seen, the created order does not merely consist in the physical reality of man and the world, but in the functional reality of both as the icon and sanctuary of God. From a theological point of view, the flood signifies that the deity has vacated creation as his sanctuary. And from an anthropological point of view, the flood signifies that man has ceased to be an icon of the deity. For this reason, those who perished in the flood serve as representatives of the human race: they are the firstfruits of sin grown to ripeness; in them, the deity places the whole of fallen creation under the sentence of death.

But while the flood amounts to a reversal of creation, the submersion and re-emersion of the ark amounts to its re-creation: *In [the ark] only a few people, eight in all, were saved through water, and this water symbolizes baptism that now saves you also* (I Pet. 3:20-21). As this passage indicates, the ark's journey through the waters of the flood provides the earliest example of the covenant initiation ritual known as baptism. Moreover, it portrays this covenant initiation ritual as a re-enactment of creation: in the submersion of the ark, man and the world die as entities sustained by creation; and in the re-emersion of the ark, they are reborn as entities sustained by covenant. In turn, this initial re-enactment of creation serves as a prototype for its repetition in the various stages of redemption that are to follow: the baptism of man as a race (in the ark) prefigures the baptism of man as a nation (in Israel) and the baptism of man as an individual (in Christ). In each of these repetitions, the deity moves through successive stages in the re-creation of man and the world.

At its deepest level, however, the ark not only preserves man and the world on behalf of the covenant, but also carries within itself the very means of their eventual redemption. The preservation of one righteous man (Gen. 6:9) and the preservation seven of every pure animal (Gen. 7:2) are both undertaken in preparation for the institution of sacrificial worship. Thus, sacrifice is revealed as the deity's chosen vehicle for redemption: it is to be the means whereby he will re-create man as his icon and the world as his sanctuary. The seven pairs of pure animals serve as the remote ancestors of the animals who will be sacrificed under the Old Covenant (purity being the quality that renders them ritually fit for sacrifice), and the man of righteousness serves as the remote ancestor of the Lamb of God who will be sacrificed under the New Covenant (righteousness being the quality that renders him morally fit for sacrifice). In the chapters that follow, we shall have a good deal more to say about the meaning of sacrificial worship, as well as about the distinction between ritual purity and moral purity. For the present, however, it is sufficient to note that all of these elements are contained within the ark, whereby it serves as the vessel for the redemption of the whole world.

The Flood as a Precedent for Divine Law

As the flood narrative draws to a conclusion, the deity's act of preserving creation on behalf of his covenant is passed into divine law. As before, he brings forth life from the depths of the sea, and his decision to re-create is rendered legally binding by virtue of an oath in which he promises to provide for the continuance of the earth and its creatures: *Never again will I doom the earth because of man, even though every inclination of his heart is evil from childhood. And never again will I destroy all living creatures as I have done* (Gen. 8:21).

As part of this divine law, the deity's promise to preserve life is accompanied by two commands: first, a reiteration of the old command to bring forth new life; and second, a new command to respect the sanctity of that life. The appearance of this new command owes to one of the most important developments in the history of man: namely, his transformation from a peaceful creature into a beast of prey. While in the garden man's hunger was amply provided for, in the land of exile he was compelled to kill for food. In the process, he incurred a tremendous life-debt, but nevertheless continued to be driven onward by an equally tremendous life-need. And thus, the human race devolved into a creature quite different from that which it was intended to be: a ruin of the divine image whose survival had been salvaged from the shipwreck of existence only by fleeing from the deity and preying upon the life of his fellow creatures.

In promising to preserve life, the deity grants man continuance in his acquired mode of existence, but in commanding man to respect the sanctity of that life he places it under certain limitations: he is forbidden to take the life of his fellow man, and he is granted only limited access to the life of the animal. Thus, even though all men have incurred a life-debt, their life stands under the protection of God: *From each man, I will demand an accounting for the life of his fellow man: whoever sheds the blood of man, by man shall his blood be shed, for in the image of God has God made man* (Gen. 9:4-6). And even though man is permitted to satisfy his life-need by taking from animal flesh, he is required to abstain from animal blood: *Just as I gave you the green plants, I now give you everything: every creature that lives will be food for you… But you must not eat meat that has its lifeblood still in it* (Gen. 9:3-4).

Ultimately, the granting of access to flesh, the prohibition of blood, and the encouraging of reproduction all pave the way for the redemption of man through the institution of sacrificial worship. For the sacrificial act consists above all in the provision of flesh for food, in the provision of blood for atonement, and in the binding together of all who partake of these elements into a single family. In these provisions we find an important clue to the perennial question of how the slaughter of a living creature can be regarded as a pious and redemptive act. For although man is uniquely made in the divine image, the various elements of this ritual reveal a deep kinship between him and the animal. Both are composed of a created element (i.e., the dust of the earth) as well as an uncreated element (i.e., the breath of life), whereby both stand at a point of intersection between the realms of the earthly and the divine. As such, the living creature is uniquely suited to serve as a medium of exchange between man and God: the flesh of the animal serving as a currency appropriate to man and providing him with food for his life-need (Lev. 3:11); and the blood of the animal serving as a currency appropriate to the deity and providing him with payment for man's life-debt (Lev. 17:11). God himself, upon whom every creature's right to life depends, sanctions this sacrificial exchange as a way of redeeming mankind: by means of its blood, he atones for man's life; by means of its flesh, he feeds man body; and through both of these acts he provides a new basis for kinship in the sharing of the sacrificial meal. As a result, the deity once more brings forth living creatures upon the earth: now, however, they are sustained not only by the vegetable food he has provided in creation, but also by the sacrificial food he has willed to provide in his covenant.

The Kingdom of God in the Old and the New Testaments

Although man has been preserved, he has not been redeemed as an icon of God: Noah's eating of the fruit of the vine, his subsequent nakedness, and the ensuing curse is clearly a repetition of the elements of the fall (Gen. 9:18-28). And although the world has been preserved, it has not been redeemed as a sanctuary of God: as the breath of the deity moved over the waters looking for a place to rest (Gen. 1:2), so the dove sent from the ark flew back and forth over the waters, but could not find a place to rest its feet (Gen. 8:8-12).

Nevertheless, the task of redemption is not something that man has it in his power to accomplish. He does not have what it takes to redeem himself or the world, but must wait upon the intervention of the Lord. To be sure, man can strive after relationship with God, but for all his ability to understand truth, for all his ability to achieve goodness, for all his ability to experience beauty, he cannot render himself fit for an encounter with God, much less provide the one condition necessary for such an encounter to occur: God himself. God alone is in a position to give himself to man: he must initiate the relationship, and man at his uttermost can only respond.

In the Bible, the promise of such an event is first given to Abraham, and he may therefore be regarded as the patriarchal ancestor of the Kingdom of God. Accordingly, both he and his descendents were marked for adoption into the divine family, inwardly by their faith in that promise (Gen. 15:6), and outwardly by their obedience to the command to undergo circumcision (Gen. 17:10). Unique among the patriarchs, the life of this remarkable man foreshadows the whole story of redemption. His food came from a barren land (Gen. 12:10), his offspring came from a barren womb (Gen. 11:30), and the binding of his son was an anticipation of the sacrificial redemption of mankind which we see inaugurated in the Passover and completed in the Crucifixion (Gen. 22). Nevertheless, none of the patriarchs lived to see the fulfillment of that for which they had hoped, since the mark of their adoption could only be redeemed at that time when the deity would prepare them for the visitation of his presence. According to the scripture, this divine act of preparation and visitation occurred in two places to which we must now turn: the Old Covenant under Moses and the New Covenant under Jesus Christ.

The Redemption of the Icon

Although the Old Testament and the New Testament are sometimes portrayed as opposed to one another, the foregoing indicates that both should be viewed as stages in the advancement of the Kingdom of God. Thus, the Kingdom of God is prepared for in the universal covenant under Noah, initiated in the national covenant under Moses, and brought to completion in the international covenant under Jesus Christ.

As the Kingdom of God achieved its first expression in creation, so it now achieves expression in his covenantal rule over the sea. In all three of the aforementioned stages of the covenant, each new phase is portrayed as a re-enactment of the creation of the world. For example, we may compare the parting of the waters in the flood story, the parting of the waters in the exodus story, and Jesus' submersion and re-emersion from the waters of baptism (an event in which the dove released from the ark at last finds a place to rest its feet [Matt. 3:16, Mk 1:10, Luke 3:21, John 1:32]). In Jesus' ministry, he demonstrates his authority over the primeval sea through his silencing of the storm (Mk 4:39), but also through his silencing of the demonic power it exercises over human life (Mk 1:25)—he is the herald of the new heaven and the new earth: the abode in which "there is no sea" (Rev. 20:1).

But how does this re-creation of man and the world come about? We have already said that the redemption of man comes about through sacrifice. The deity's creational rule over the sea began with his breathing into his creatures the breath of life, making the earth productive of food, and making the womb productive of offspring. And in the same way, his covenantal rule over the sea begins with his provision of atonement through sacrificial blood, his provision of food through sacrificial flesh, and his begetting of offspring through the sacrificial meal. Herein consists the redemption of man, but it must nevertheless be for a specific purpose, and so our attention is drawn once more to the role that he is intended to play in the sanctuary of God.

The Redemption of the Sanctuary

Man is redeemed as the deity's icon in order that he might be brought back into the deity's sanctuary, to reflect his divine glory, and to enter into his divine rest: *I will put my tent among you, and I will not abhor you. I will walk among you and be your God, and you will be my people* (Lev. 26:11-12).

In the Old Covenant under Moses, an external sanctuary for the deity's presence is provided in the temple. In the New Covenant under Jesus Christ, an internal sanctuary for the deity's presence is provided in the soul of the believer: *Jesus declared, "Believe me, a time is coming when you will worship the Father neither on this mountain nor in Jerusalem. You Samaritans worship what you do not know; we worship what we do know, for salvation is from the Jews. Yet a time is coming and has now come when the true worshippers will worship the Father in spirit and in truth, for they are the kind of worshippers the Father seeks"* (John 4:21-23).

From a practical point of view, this means that what took place outwardly in the temple is to take place inwardly in the life of the believer: most notably, the indwelling of the divine presence. For this very reason, the scriptures retain a very detailed record of the laws and rituals of temple worship: they are not obsolete, nor are they merely of historical interest, but they are a map of the human soul and of the life of worship that is to be conducted within the human soul. Thus, while it is clear that the present day believer does not observe these laws and rituals outwardly, they are nevertheless intended to understand, practice, and experience them inwardly. By entering this interior life of worship, the believer need not fear that they are abandoning faith and turning toward the works of the law. For it is by faith that this interior life of worship is made possible, not as a command we must obey in order to be justified, but as a promise of blessing we have received through our justification. Moreover, it is the organ through which our beliefs are translated into experience, in order that grace may not simply be acknowledged with our heads, but applied to our hearts. In short, it is through the interior life of worship that the power of grace is released and made effectual for the sanctification of the believer.

CHAPTER TWO

The Garden, the Temple, and the Christ

Then have them make a sanctuary for me,
and I will dwell among them.

Exodus 25:8

God is spirit, but man is spirit in the world. Therefore, if God is going to be in communion with man, he must enter the world at a certain place and at a certain time in order that man may have access to him. Such places and times are called sanctuaries and the scriptures present us with two primary classes of them: first, a creational prototype, found in the Garden of Eden; and second, three covenantal expressions of this prototype, found in the Tabernacle, the person of Jesus Christ, and the souls of the individuals who make up his Church.

The creational sanctuary is the ideal. In the aftermath of man's rebellion, the three covenantal forms of the sanctuary mark progressive stages in the redemption of this ideal: in the Tabernacle, the deity reveals to man his estrangement from the Father; in Christ, the deity reveals to man his reconciliation through the Son; and in the Church, the deity reveals to man his redemption as the temple of the Holy Spirit. In all of these various expressions, however, the basic function of the sanctuary remains the same: to serve as the seat of God's kingship, the place where he meets with man, and the place where he speaks his word to his people—it is a palace, a temple, and an oracle.

This then is the high destiny of the human soul. In its fallen condition, however, it has become a vacated sanctuary, and has by default been converted into a warehouse for the trinkets of the world. As a result, man's psychological life is often characterized by a profound sense of vocation, but also by an equally profound sense of triviality, futility, and emptiness. His redemption from this wretched condition consists in the recovery of the deity's infinite presence, whereby he also recovers the one meaningful point of reference for all of the finite things that make up his world. Most important of all, however, when at last the treasure of the deity's presence achieves a domicile in this fragile jar of clay, the created order is able once more to serve as the icon and sanctuary of YHWH.

The Garden Sanctuary

In Genesis, YHWH creates and then he rests. In the previous chapter, we have seen that the idea of rest not only indicates that God rests from his work, but also that God rests within his work: *And God blessed the seventh day and made it holy, because on it he rested from all the work of creating that he had done* (Gen. 2:3).

Throughout the remainder of the book, we find no other mention of the word "holy." From other passages of scripture, however, we learn that when the presence of the deity comes to rest in a particular place, he communicates his holiness to the spatial and temporal dimensions of that place, thereby transforming it into a sanctuary: *YHWH said to Moses, "Do not come any closer. Remove your sandals from your feet, for the place on which you stand is holy ground* (Ex. 3:5).

The first place of this kind is the Garden of Eden. Although research into the name of this place indicates that it denotes abundance, its precise location remains a mystery. Nevertheless, the most significant element in the makeup of this earthly paradise is not to be sought in the fact of its material richness, but in the fact that it served as a resting place for God. Indeed, in the other passages of scripture where we find it mentioned, it is simply referred to as the "garden of God" (Gen. 13:10, Is. 51:3, Ezek. 28:13).

The Garden before the Fall

In the previous chapter, I said that the whole of creation was designed to serve as a sanctuary, comparable to the Tabernacle of Moses. At this point, I would like to take the comparison one step further and suggest that we are able to observe a threefold division of the garden corresponding to the three fold division of the Tabernacle: that is, to the Most Holy Place, the Holy Place, and the Outer Court.

In the Tabernacle, the Most Holy Place was the part of the sanctuary where the presence of the deity rested. In the garden, this place is identified with a great subterranean stream from which God watered the Garden of Eden (Gen. 2:10-14). He is therefore present in the garden at the hidden source of all its earthly abundance, a theme that later appears in connection with the temple (Ps. 46:4). On the basis of such passages, YHWH's presence eventually acquires poetic significance as "the spring of living water" (Jer. 2:13).

As for the Holy Place, this was the part of the sanctuary where the deity bestowed upon man the gifts that flowed out from his presence. In the temple these were found in the menorah and the table of bread, while in the garden they are found in the corresponding images of the tree of life and the gift of food. Throughout the Bible, we find numerous instances of this pairing of light with food, suggesting an important connection about which more will be said later. For the present, it is sufficient to note that the deity's presence acquires poetic significance as "the bread of life" and also as "the light of life" (Ps. 119:103-104).

As for the Outer Court, this was the part of the sanctuary reserved for sacrificial worship, and is therefore encountered only after the fall (see the following section). If we take the account of man's creation together with that of his life in the garden-sanctuary, we are immediately struck by the variety of different ways the deity's presence is communicated to him: it is present to him in the breath of life (Gen. 2:7); it is present to him in the water of life (Gen. 2:10); and it is present to him in the tree and the fruit and the word of life (Gen. 2:16). In short, YHWH has become incarnate in creation, just as he would later do in the temple, and just as he would later do in the person of Jesus Christ. And in turn, this creational sanctuary provides a resting place for man, who, though mortal, is sustained by the life of God: *Blessed is the one who trusts in YHWH, whose trust alone is YHWH. He shall be like a tree planted by waters, that sends out its roots by a stream. It does not fear when heat comes; its leaves are always green. It has no worries in years of drought and never fails to bear fruit* (Jer. 17:7-8). *But cursed is the one who trusts in man, who depends on flesh for his strength and turns his thoughts from YHWH. He will be like a bush in the desert; he will not see prosperity when it comes. He will dwell in the parched places of the desert, in a salt land where no one lives* (Jer. 17:5-6).

The Garden after the Fall

The foregoing passage mentions a blessing as well as a curse, and it is easy to see that we cannot have one without at least the possibility of the other. As man's union with the deity entails blessedness, so his falling away from the deity entails a curse. Accordingly, the fall occasions a whole new dynamic in the arrangement of the sanctuary: although the previous elements remain, they are transformed in such a way as to reflect the mutual hostility between the sinfulness of man and the holiness of God.

Now the deity manifests himself in the appearance of a fiery sword (Gen. 3:24). From this point forward, his holy presence will continue to express itself in one or another form resembling fire: to Abraham, it appears as a blazing torch under a smoking firepot (Gen. 15:17); to Moses, it appears as flames of fire from within a bush (Ex. 3:2); and to the Israelites, it appears as a pillar of fire by night and a pillar of cloud by day (Ex. 13:21). Accompanying him are the "cherubim," mythic creatures widely recognized in antiquity and regarded as the guardians of sacred space—in this case, the resting place of the deity, whose presence is no longer depicted as a life-giving stream, but as a life-consuming flame.

According to the biblical text, mankind is said to have been driven east of the Garden of Eden (Gen. 3:24). Here, our attention is drawn to the fact that the doorways on the floor-plan of the sanctuary were always stationed to the east (Ex. 27:13-14). In other words, as man moved along an eastward trajectory, he moved by stages farther and farther away from the presence of God, so that his expulsion from the garden in effect moves him from the Holy Place to the Outer Court. Accordingly, it is at this point that the narrative introduces the practice of sacrificial worship in the story of Cain and Abel (the courtyard being the location of the sacrificial altar, Gen. 4:3-4). Man now approaches the deity from a safe distance, and then only through the mediation of a sacrificial offering, in acknowledgement of the fact that the food sustaining his life has been bought through the payment of his life-debt.

As the story of the fall continues, man's sin against the deity ripens into sin against his brother, and the human family is banished to the east once more: this time away from the land of Eden and into the land of Nod (Gen. 4:16). As Eden connotes home, Nod connotes wandering, suggesting man's transition from a life of rest to a life of restlessness. And as mentioned in the previous chapter, this restlessness consists in a continual flight from the deity's presence (whereby man seeks to escape his life-debt), and in a continual search for food (whereby man seeks to satisfy his life-need). *Now you are driven from [my presence]... You will be a restless wanderer on the earth, and the ground will no longer yield its crops for you* (Gen. 4:11-12). Man in his brokenness has been removed from the sanctuary altogether, cast adrift in a world vacated by God. It is here, in the midst of his exile from the city of God, that he inaugurates the project of human civilization, a project that eventually culminates in the archetypal city of Babel, and in the historical empires of Egypt, Babylon, and Rome: *Cain went out from YHWH's presence and lived in the land of Nod, east of Eden... And then he founded a city, and he named it after his son* (Gen. 4:16-17).

The Tabernacle Sanctuary

As mentioned, the Kingdom of God is redeemed by virtue of a historical covenant that unfolds in three different stages. In the first stage of this covenant, the deity preserves man and the world, but in the second stage of the covenant he undertakes the sacrificial redemption of both. This work of sacrificial redemption is promised to the patriarch Abraham, inaugurated in the Old Israel under Moses, and brought to completion in the New Israel under Christ.

Like the story of creation, the story of the covenant begins in a garden. Now, however, we are not speaking of the garden of God, but of the false imitations of it manufactured by man. Noah's vineyard was the first of these, and the events that occurred there mirror the events of the fall. From this point forward, it is not in the garden but in the desert that man must wait for the revelation of the deity. Man-made paradises are surrogates for the divine presence, but the desert is the place where the deity re-enacts the work of creation: *YHWH will surely comfort Zion and will look with compassion on all her ruins; he will make her deserts like Eden, her wastelands like the garden of YHWH* (Is. 51:3).

In the Old Testament, man's journey of redemption begins with the story of Israel's exodus from Egypt. In appearance, it was a garden-sanctuary: teeming with gods, and the flower of human civilization. But in reality it was a counterfeit: its gods were idols and its civilization was built on human enslavement. Therefore, YHWH instructs Moses to lead Israel out of this man-made paradise and into the wastelands of the desert. In the desert, man would be re-created; his life-debt would be paid and his life-need would be filled; he would die as a creature dependent upon creation, and be reborn as a creature dependent upon covenant: *Remember how YHWH your God led you all the way in the desert these forty years... He humbled you, causing you to hunger and then feeding you with manna, which neither you nor your fathers had known, to teach you that man does not live by bread alone but on every word that comes from the mouth of God* (Deut. 8:2-3).

The Redemption of Old Israel

The redemption of Israel consists in three events: the Passover, the Exodus, and the giving of both the Torah and the Tabernacle at Mt. Sinai. Although these three events exhibit a rich variety of historical detail, the substance of the story they tell is clear: YHWH re-enters creation to redeem his firstborn son, he brings his children out of the land of bondage, and he establishes a new way of life for them in the sanctuary of his presence.

In the Passover, YHWH re-enters creation to redeem his firstborn son. But because the holiness of the deity now stands opposed to the sinfulness of man, this divine visitation is one for which man must make special preparation. As the deity moves throughout the land in search of his firstborn son, he inevitably endangers the lives of all the firstborn in Egypt. Therefore, YHWH prepares his people by instructing them to have their homes ritually purified, and he redeems them by atoning for them with sacrificial blood and feeding them with sacrificial food. As we shall see, this threefold requirement of purification, sacrificial atonement, and the sharing of a sacrificial meal establishes the basic dynamic of the relationship between man and God.

In the Exodus, YHWH brings his children out of the land of bondage. In YHWH's parting of the waters of the sea, the adoption of his children achieves poetic expression as a fresh re-enactment of creation. Once again, he is king over the flood, using it as an instrument of his justice and grace. In his justice, he uses the sea to swallow up the armies of Egypt: *Sing to YHWH, for he is highly exalted. The horse and its rider he has hurled into the sea* (Ex. 15:1). And in his grace, he saves a remnant for redemption from the creature of the sea: *Was it not you who cut Rahab to pieces, who pierced that monster through? Was it not you who died up the sea, the waters of the great deep, who made a road in the depths of the sea so that the ransomed might cross over?* (Is. 51:9-10). Most important of all, however, in leading his people through the waters of the sea, he brings them out of the garden of man and into the desert of YHWH: *I remember the devotion of your youth, how as a bride you loved me and followed me through the desert, through a land not sown. Israel was holy to YHWH, the firstfruits of his harvest; all who devoured her were held guilty, and disaster overtook them* (Jer. 2:2-3).

As the story draws to a close, the deity's act of redeeming his people is passed into divine law with the giving of the Torah and the Tabernacle at Mt. Sinai. Here, in the desert, we at last come to the point where the deity actually begins to re-create man and the world: in the Torah, he begins the process of redeeming man as an icon of God; and in the Tabernacle, he begins the process of redeeming the world as a sanctuary of God. Nevertheless, while his kingdom is inaugurated here, it is not brought to completion here. For the Torah requires that its commands be obeyed in order for the promise of the kingdom to be fulfilled. If Israel should prove obedient to these commands, then the promise of the kingdom would be realized: *If you follow my laws and faithfully observe my commandments... I will put my dwelling among you, and I will not abhor you* (Lev. 26:3-13). But if Israel should prove disobedient to these commands, then the promise of the kingdom would not be realized: *But if you do not obey me and do not observe all these commandments... I will set my face against you* (Lev. 26:14-46). And the promise of the kingdom was this: that she should be made perfect in her communion with the deity and become a source of salvation for the whole world: *Now if you obey me fully and keep my covenant, then out of all nations you will be my treasured possession. Although the whole earth is mine, you will be for me [a holy nation] and [a kingdom of priests]* (Ex. 19:5-6).

The Tabernacle of Moses

The preceding gives us a picture of the inauguration of the Kingdom of God. The supreme law of this kingdom is the Torah, but the spatial and temporal center out of which this kingdom operates is the Tabernacle: the abode of the divine presence and the place where Israel enjoys communion with YHWH.

In the Tabernacle, we find a combination of the imagery of the garden both before and after the fall, suggesting its role as a mediator between the rival claims of holiness and sin. In the Most Holy Place, we once more find the cherubim guarding access to the divine presence, which manifests itself in the form of a consuming fire. In the Holy Place, the golden altar of incense stands in perpetual supplication of the deity, while the tree-shaped menorah and its accompaniments of light and food stand as symbols of the gifts man enjoys through his communion with God. And in the Outer Court, man's approach to the deity is facilitated by the laver (providing him with water for purification) and the altar (providing him with blood for atonement and flesh for food).

In turn, the imagery of the sanctuary points to the fundamental purpose of the law: that is, to render man fit to enter into the presence of YHWH. In the first place, he is rendered fit by virtue of his obedience to its commands: *Who may ascend the hill of YHWH? Who may stand in his holy place? He who has clean hands and a pure heart, who does not lift up his soul to an idol or swear by what is false* (Ps. 24:3-4). But in the second place, he is rendered fit by virtue of its provision for restoration through the blood of the altar and the water of the laver: *Have mercy on me, O God. According to your faithfulness, according to your abundant compassion, blot out my transgressions. Wash away all my iniquity, and purify me from my sin* (Ps. 51:1-2).

Nevertheless, while the realization of the covenant promise begins here, it is not brought to completion here. Although the Tabernacle provides access to the divine presence, it does so only on a local and temporal basis. And while the Torah provides a promise of perfect blessedness, it does so only on the condition of perfect purity and obedience. True, in the absence of perfect purity and obedience, it provides a system of atonement whereby man can be continually brought back into communion with God. Nevertheless, these repeated acts of restoration do not satisfy the requirements of purity and obedience as much as they sustain man in spite of his inability to meet them. Thus, sanctuary worship has the paradoxical effect of augmenting the gap between the sinfulness of man and the holiness of God: *The Torah was given so that the trespass might increase* (Rom. 5:20). While it is indeed an authentic form of worship, it expresses itself in a continuing cycle of approach and withdrawal, just as a butterfly moves to and fro in the presence of a flame: *The Holy Spirit was showing by this that the way into the Most Holy Place had not yet been disclosed as long as the first Tabernacle was still standing. This is an illustration for the present time, indicating that the gifts and sacrifices being offered were not able to clear the conscience of the worshipper. They are only a matter of food and drink and various ceremonial washings—external regulations applying until the time of the new order* (Heb. 9:8-10).

The Christ Sanctuary

In the book of Hebrews, Moses, the Torah, and the Tabernacle are all described as "a copy and a shadow of the good things that are coming" (Heb. 10:1). The Kingdom of God is initiated in the Old Covenant under Moses, but it is brought to completion in the New Covenant under Jesus Christ.

In the story of Moses, we saw how the land of Egypt was

compared to the Garden of Eden, how earthly paradise had become a symbol for the absence of God. This same theme recurs in Isaiah's *Song of the Vineyard*, only now it is the nation of Israel that has become a garden without God (Is. 5:1-7). Jesus takes up this theme in his *Parable of the Tenants* (Mk. 12:1-12): just as Israel was called out of Egypt into the desert, so Jesus' ministry is preceded by a call to leave Israel and to go into the desert once more. The Gospel of Matthew reads: *In those days John the Baptist came, preaching in the desert of Judea and saying, "Repent, for the kingdom of heaven is near." This is he who was spoken of through Isaiah the prophet: A voice of one calling the desert, "Prepare the way for the Lord, make straight paths for him"* (Matt. 3:1-3).

As before, this call into the desert was a call to death and rebirth, a call to even deeper dependence on the covenant. Now, however, the call was away from the old Israel and into the new Israel, away from the outward and temporal and into the inward and eternal. *"The time is coming," declares YHWH, "when I will make a new covenant with the house of Israel and with the house of Judah. It will not be like the covenant I made with their forefathers when I took them by the hand to lead them out of Egypt, because they broke my covenant, though I was a husband to them," declares YHWH. "This is the covenant I will make with the house of Israel after that time," declares YHWH. "I will put my Torah in their minds and write it on their hearts. I will be their God, and they will be my people. No longer will a man teach his neighbor, or a man his brother, saying, 'Know YHWH,' because they all will know me, form the least of them to the greatest," declares YHWH. "For I will forgive their iniquity and will remember their sin no more"* (Jer. 31:31-34).

The Redemption of the New Israel

In the Torah, Moses foretells the coming of a prophet like himself: *YHWH your God will raise up for you a prophet like me from among your own brothers* (Deut. 18:15). Nevertheless, at a later point the text says: *Since then, no prophet has risen in Israel like Moses, whom YHWH knew face to face* (Deut. 34:10). The New Testament portrays Jesus as the fulfillment of this ancient prophecy, a second deliverer who would inaugurate a greater Passover, lead his people through a greater Exodus, and establish for them a greater Torah and Tabernacle.

Jesus' Passover occurs at the end of his earthly ministry, and is the means whereby he shares the kingdom that has been fulfilled in himself with others. He fulfills the kingdom within himself because he is perfectly obedient to the commands of the Torah and is in himself the incarnation of the Tabernacle. And he shares the kingdom with others through his sacrificial death, whereby he offers the gift of his blood to purify their souls from sin, and whereby he offers the gift of his body to feed their souls with the indwelling presence of God. He is the new Passover Lamb: *For you know that it was not with perishable things that you were redeemed from the empty way of life handed down to you from your forefathers, but with the precious blood of Christ, a lamb without blemish or defect. He was chosen before the creation of the world, but was revealed in these last times for your sake* (I Pet. 1:18-20).

Jesus' Exodus, therefore, is not a liberation from enslavement to any earthly ruler, but a liberation from enslavement to sin. As the first phase of the covenant was marked by man's passage through the waters of the flood, and as the second phase of the covenant was marked by his passage through the waters of the sea, so the third phase of the covenant is marked by his passage through the waters of baptism. Jesus' submersion and re-emersion from the waters of baptism signifies his work of death and resurrection, and it indicates that the effect of this work is applied to all who enter the waters of baptism with him. While for Jesus' followers baptism is an act of repentance, for him it is an act of self-giving: he becomes the ark, the vessel in which fallen humanity is carried through the waters of destruction: *We were therefore buried with him through baptism into death in order that, just as Christ was raised from the dead through the glory of the Father, we too might live a new life* (Rom. 6:4).

Jesus' baptism and temptation in the desert is immediately followed by the inauguration of his public ministry: *The time is fulfilled; the Kingdom of God has come near; repent, and believe the good news* (Mark 1:15). In his person, he is the incarnation of the sanctuary: *The word became flesh and tabernacled among us. We have seen his glory, the glory of the One and Only, who came from the Father, full of grace and truth* (John 1:14). And in his work, he endeavors to transform individuals into his likeness, into sanctuaries indwelt by the presence of God: *For those God foreknew he also predestined to be conformed to the likeness of his Son, that he might be the firstborn among many brothers* (Rom. 8:29). A soul thus transformed is a palace, a temple, and an oracle, a province within the Kingdom of God: *The Kingdom of God does not come with your careful observation, nor will people say 'Here it is,' or 'There it is,' because the Kingdom of God is within you* (Luke 17:20-21). And a soul thus transformed is ruled through the governance of its sovereign king: *And I will put my Spirit in you. Thus, I will cause you to follow my laws and faithfully observe my decrees* (Ezek. 36:27).

The Tabernacle of Christ

In Jesus' preaching at the temple, he uses a number of metaphors to identify himself with the sanctuary. He is one with the divine presence: *I and the Father are one* (John 10:30). He is the stream of living water: *Whoever believes in me, as the Scripture has said, streams of living water will flow from within him* (John 7:38). He is the tree of life: *I am the true vine, and my Father is the gardener* (John 15:1). He is the gift of light: *I am the light of the world* (John 8:12). And he is the gift of food: *I am the bread of life* (John 6:35).

As mentioned, Jesus' work is to transform the souls of his disciples into sanctuaries, and there is no more concrete expression for what a sanctuary is than that found in the Tabernacle of Moses. It is for this reason that we are able to regard the Tabernacle as a "map of the human soul." It provides us with a description not only of the inner person of Christ, but of the inner life that the disciple is intended to enjoy through Christ. It is the interpretive key that unlocks the door to the mystical dimension of human life we find revealed in the scriptures.

On the basis of the foregoing, we are now in a position to say more precisely what this imagery means. If the soul is a sanctuary, then it is first and foremost a place for the indwelling of the presence of God: *Don't you know that you yourselves are God's temple and that God's spirit lives in you* (I Cor. 3:16). If the soul is a sanctuary, then it is a place where prayer rises as incense before God: *May my prayer be set before you like incense; may the lifting up of my hands be like the evening sacrifice* (Ps. 141:2). If the soul is a sanctuary, then it is a place where prayerful communion brings light: *[Jesus said] "I am the light of the world. Whoever follows me will never walk in darkness, but will have the light of life* (John 8:12). If the soul is a sanctuary, then it is a place where prayerful communion brings food: *Jesus declared, "I am the bread of life. He who comes to me will never go hungry, and he who believes in me will never be thirsty* (John 6:35).

This is the center of the life of discipleship. When Jesus calls us to follow him, he calls us to follow him in his inner person. Our following is an inward following, an obedience that is not manifested in this or that outward act, but an obedience that is manifested in the more fundamental actions and transactions of the heart. Accordingly, the organ of this obedience is faith: *Then they asked him, "What must we do to do the works God requires?" Jesus answered, "The work of God is this: to believe in the one he has sent"* (John 6:28-29). As an organ of obedience, faith is not only a belief, but also an activity: namely, that of fixing they eye of the mind upon the divine presence, and of entering into a life of perpetual worship before God: *One thing I ask of YHWH, this is what I seek: that I may dwell in the house of YHWH all the days of my life, to gaze upon the beauty of YHWH and to seek him in his temple* (Ps. 27:4).

CHAPTER THREE

The Sanctuary of the Human Soul

*Observe my Sabbaths and have reverence
for my sanctuary. I am YHWH.*

Leviticus 19:30

The basic theme of the scriptures is the Kingdom of God: established at creation, restored in his covenant, and manifested in his sanctuary. In the previous chapter, we saw that the sanctuary appears in four different forms: the creational form of the Garden of Eden, and the three covenantal forms of the Tabernacle of Moses, the person of Jesus Christ, and the souls of the disciples who make up his Church.

Once this basic point is grasped, ancient temple worship acquires practical significance for the modern believer, for it provides a copy and a shadow of the worship that is to be conducted in the human soul. Man was created in order that he might reflect the glory of God by worshipping God: that is, by knowing him, serving him, and enjoying him forever. It is in this interior life of knowing, serving, and enjoying that man fulfills his divinely appointed vocation as the icon and sanctuary of God.

At its most elementary level, this worship involves not only the sanctuary, but also three additional elements: the acts that occur within it; the agents who perform those acts, and the relation of these agents to the surrounding spatial-temporal world. These three elements provide the foundation for all that follows, which may be said to consist in an exposition of the spiritual life of worship as conducted within the sanctuary of the human soul.

The Initial Act

Although there are many acts that take place within the sanctuary, the most important is deity's indwelling of it with his holy presence, manifested in the form of a consuming fire. Every other act that occurs in the sanctuary is established on the foundation of this one original act. Apart from this, there is no divine presence, no sanctuary, and no true worship, even in the midst of a host of apparent signs of religious vitality. In ancient Israel, for example, the temple remained operative long after the divine presence had vacated it. And in the same way, the church of today can engage in all manner of religious activities in the absence of any genuine spiritual presence.

In the Old Testament, the first act of indwelling occurred in the Tabernacle: *Then the cloud covered the Tent of Meeting, and the glory of YHWH filled the Tabernacle. Moses could not enter the Tent of Meeting, because the cloud had settled on it, and the glory of YHWH filled the Tabernacle* (Ex. 40:34-35). This act was then repeated at the dedication of the first temple: *When the priests withdrew from the Holy Place, the cloud filled the temple of YHWH. And the priests could not perform their service because of the cloud, for the glory of YHWH filled his temple* (I Kgs 8:10-11). Significantly, however, this act was not repeated at the building of the second temple, a fact which foreshadowed the imminent relocation of the divine presence in the person of Jesus Christ: *Who of you is left who saw this house in its former glory? How does it look to you now? Does it not seem to you like nothing? But now be strong... For I am with you... This is what I covenanted with you when you came out of Egypt... In a little while I will once more shake the heavens and the earth... The glory of this latter house will be greater than the glory of the former house... And in this place I will grant peace* (Hagg. 2:3-9).

In the New Testament, a desperate attempt was made to fulfill this prophetic expectation through the material refurbishing of the temple: *As [Jesus] was leaving the temple, one of his disciples said to him "Look, Teacher! What massive stones! What magnificent buildings!"* (Mk 13:1). Jesus, however, indicates that it is not in its material grandeur, but in the indwelling of the divine presence that the true glory of the temple lies: the temple that has been vacated will be destroyed: *"Do you see all these great buildings?" replied Jesus. "Not one stone here will be left on another; every one will be thrown down"* (Mk 13:2); but the temple that has been inhabited will prove indestructible: *Jesus answered them, "Destroy this temple, and I will raise it again in three days"* (John 2:19). In making these claims, Jesus indicates that the indwelling of the divine presence has occurred in his own person: *The Word became flesh and made his dwelling among us* (John 1:14). Furthermore, through his sacrificial death and resurrection, he shares the divine presence with his disciples: *[The disciples] saw what appeared to be tongues of fire that separated and came to rest on each one of them. All of them were filled with the Holy Spirit and began to speak in other tongues as the Spirit enabled them* (Acts 2:3-4). In this event, man enters into real communion with God: his religious striving does not consist in a valiant search for one who is absent, but in gently seeking the face of the one who has made himself present. God is no longer just an object of theoretical belief, or of practical motivation, or even of aesthetic experience, but a living reality that has entered into organic union with the soul of man. It is a historical reality, and one for which there is a correspondingly historical awareness, for it is in the act of faith that we perceive his act of indwelling us.

The Three Agents

The three primary agents in the temple are YHWH, the priests, and the laity. YHWH is the one who dwells in the adytum of the sanctuary, the priests are those who serve in the antechamber of the sanctuary, and the laity are those who worship in the courtyard of the sanctuary.

As we have already seen, the spiritual life of worship is founded upon one fundamental act: YHWH's indwelling of the sanctuary with his holy presence. Building upon this foundation, we are now in a position to note the relationship between each of the three agents we have mentioned. First, YHWH transmits the divine quality of holiness to his priests, then his priests mediate the divine quality of holiness to the laity, and finally the laity mediates the divine quality of holiness to the world.

Here, we arrive at the heart of ancient temple worship: by living in the sanctuary of the deity, man not only reflects the divine glory, but discovers a new basis for kinship in holiness, whereby he and others are knit together into one holy community. Thus, the Kingdom of God advances as the deity's holiness spreads throughout the lives of his creatures on earth: *They will neither harm nor destroy on all my holy mountain, for the earth will be filled with the knowledge of the glory of YHWH, as the waters cover the sea* (Is. 11:9).

YHWH

YHWH is the Holy One (Heb. *Haqqadosh*). He is the one whose presence is manifested in the form of fire, the one whose presence consumes all that is contrary to it, and the one who causes his presence to dwell within the sanctuary.

As we have seen, the prototype of this act is found in creation, when he fashions the cosmos as his sanctuary and then rests within it. In each of the three phases of his historic covenant, this twofold act is repeated, with the divinity achieving greater proximity to man in each subsequent repetition.

YHWH thereby resumes his purpose at creation: to manifest his glory to the world by showing forth the fullness of his being, his goodness, and his beauty. Again, he achieves this purpose by entering into communion with man, in order that he might redeem him as a reflection of his glory, and therefore as a steward and a son of God. Thus, God indwells the sanctuary not only to reveal himself as holy, but also to transmit the quality of holiness to his people, and through his people to the nations of the world: *Now if you obey me fully and keep my covenant, then out of all nations you will be my treasured possession: [a holy nation] and [a kingdom of priests]* (Ex. 19:4-6); *I am YHWH who brought you up out of Egypt to be your God; therefore be holy, because I am holy* (Lev. 11:45).

The Priesthood and the Laity

Man is spirit in the world. When YHWH causes his spirit to dwell within the sanctuary, the divine presence is made accessible to man. By the same token, however, the sanctuary is inherently limited by its localization in space and time: it is not accessible to all men everywhere and at all times. Thus, we are confronted with a paradox: for the indwelling of the sanctuary is an event that occurs at a particular place and time, and yet it is an event whose significance is supposed to extend to the human race universally.

Herein lies the significance of the priesthood: it is the institution through which the holiness of the deity is channeled first to the nation of Israel, and then to the nations of the rest of the world. The priests are given special access to God, not only for their own sake, and not only for the sake of Israel, but for the sake of the whole world. Accordingly, appointment to the priesthood is not based on personal ambition, or social worth, but divine election. For holiness is not a quality that man has it in his power to attain, but one that he can only receive through the grace of God. The priests are not admitted into the divine presence because they are holy, but they are holy because they have been admitted into the divine presence. To be sure, the manner in which they respond to this grace is consequential: Eleazar's lineage was granted a continuing priesthood because of its loyalty (Num. 25:10-13); Ithamar's lineage was denied a continuing priesthood because of its disloyalty (I Sam. 2:27-36). Nevertheless, the office of the priesthood is first and foremost a grace, and one that carries with it not only a unique privilege, but also a unique set of responsibilities. The priests are to serve as caretakers of the sanctuary, as exemplars of the life of holiness, and as mediators of the life of holiness: *Through [the priests], those permitted near me, I will be proven holy, before all the people, I will be accorded glory* (Lev. 10:3).

In the New Testament, the priesthood fulfills this divinely appointed destiny. In Jesus Christ, the true temple and the great high priest, the sanctuary moves from a local expression to a universal expression, for he takes the divine presence within himself and relocates it within the souls of those who place their faith in him. And just as it is the destiny of every soul to become a sanctuary for the divine presence, so it is the destiny of every person to serve as a priest within the sanctuary of the divine presence. In Moses, the promise is given: *Now if you obey me fully and keep my covenant, then out of all nations you will be my treasured possession: a kingdom of priests and a holy nation* (Ex. 19:4-6). In Christ, the promise is fulfilled: *To him who loves us and has freed us from our sins by his blood, and has made us to be a kingdom and priests to serve his God and Father* (Rev. 1:5-6). Nevertheless, the duties of this new priesthood are the same as they have always been: through repeated acts of faith to cultivate the presence of God, and to serve as caretakers of the sanctuary, as exemplars of the life of the holiness, and as mediators of the life of holiness: *As you come to him, the living Stone—rejected by men, but chosen by God, and precious to him—you also, like living stones, are being built into a spiritual house to be a holy priesthood, offering spiritual sacrifices acceptable to God through Jesus Christ... You are a chosen people, a royal priesthood, a holy nation, a people belonging to God, that you may declare the praises of him who called you out of darkness into his wonderful light* (I Pet. 2:4-5, 9).

The Sanctuary in Space and Time

Although YHWH's ultimate concern is his people, the indwelling of his presence nevertheless has an effect on the medium of space and time. By virtue of the divine presence, the sanctuary becomes a sacred space, and one which encloses sacred time.

Here again, we may observe that the quality of sanctity owes entirely to the presence of the divinity. Sanctity is not a quality that can be manufactured by human activity, no matter how pious, noble, or sublime. In the absence of the presence of the divinity, man's piety, nobility, and sublimity can at best create the illusion of sanctity, and at worst serve as a substitute for it.

In the Old Testament, the priests who work in the sanctuary are understood as dwelling in the midst of sacred space and sacred time. In the New Testament, this privilege is clearly extended to the life of all believers, for they have become in themselves a temple, a priesthood, and a body of worshippers. But along with this privilege comes a corresponding responsibility, for if the believer is always living in sacred space and sacred time, then the highest requirements of holiness are incumbent upon his person and work in all places and at all times—he must live a life "worthy of the calling he has received." In both covenants, therefore, we find a set of spatial and temporal divisions that serve to demarcate the boundary between the sanctuary and the world. These spatial and temporal divisions mark the all-important frontier between the sphere of the sacred and the sphere of the common, a frontier created by the indwelling of the divine presence and maintained by the efforts of the priesthood. This frontier was not only a reality for the priesthood of old, but it remains a reality for the priesthood of believers today. If the priesthood fails to maintain the boundaries of this frontier, if the common is allowed to intrude into the sphere of the sacred, then the sanctuary will become polluted, and may ultimately be vacated by YHWH: *Son of man, do you see what they are doing—the utterly detestable things the house of Israel is doing here, things that will drive me from my sanctuary?* (Ezek. 8:6); *Then the glory of YHWH departed from over the threshold of the temple and stopped above the cherubim. While I watched, the cherubim spread their wings and rose from the ground, and as they went, the wheels went with them. They stopped at the entrance to the east gate of YHWH's house, and the glory of the God of Israel was above them* (Ezek. 10:18-19).

The Boundaries of Sacred Space

In terms of space, the aforementioned frontier between the sacred and the common is established in three parts: (1) a central part, consisting of the sanctuary itself (i.e., the Most Holy Place, the Holy Place, and the Outer Court); (2) a peripheral part, consisting of the community gathered around the sanctuary (i.e., the nation of Israel); (3) and an external part, consisting of the outside world (i.e., the nations of the Gentiles).

After the divine presence moved from Mt. Sinai into the Tabernacle, the people arranged their lives around the sanctuary and separated themselves off from the Gentiles. This arrangement was no arbitrary expression of divine favor, nor was it one of nationalist prejudice, but it was an attempt to come to grips with the real dynamics of holiness in the spatial-temporal world. From the resting place of the divine presence, the quality of holiness emanated outward in diminishing levels of sanctity. For this reason, the requirements of holiness were greatest in the immediate vicinity of the sanctuary and decreased as one moved away from it. Thus, the highest requirements of holiness were reserved for the high priest followed by the priests (Lev. 21:10-15 and Lev. 21:1-6), and then the Nazirites followed by the Israelites

(Num. 6:1-21 and Lev. 18-20), whereas none were required for the Gentiles.

This threefold division of space is reaffirmed in the New Testament. In the gospel of John, for example, we repeatedly encounter a division between Christ, the disciples, and the world. Christ is the temple par excellence: *The temple [Jesus] had spoken of was his body* (John 2:21). Christ's disciples are the community of believers who have been taken from the world and who have gathered around him as their sanctuary: *I have revealed you to those whom you gave me out of the world* (John 17:6). And the nations of the world are understood as consisting of those who remain alienated from the community of believers and their God: *I am not praying for the world, but for those you have given me, for they are yours* (John 17:1-26). In other words, the fact that there is a real presence of the divinity that comes to rest in the soul of the believer indicates that the dynamics of sacred space remain in effect. Indeed, they are not less potent but more potent, for sacred space can be said to extend to all believers everywhere, inasmuch as they carry it inside of them wherever they go. By the same token, however, all believers everywhere are bound to the highest standards of holiness, for they are a priesthood dwelling in the presence of a holy God. They must therefore avoid pollution by the world and cultivate a life of holiness: *Religion that God our Father accepts as pure and faultless is this: to look after orphans and widows in their distress and to keep oneself from being polluted by the world* (James 1:27); *Since we have these promises, dear friends, let us purify ourselves from everything that contaminates body and spirit, perfecting holiness in the fear of God* (II Cor. 7:1).

The Boundaries of Sacred Time

As with sacred space, so there are three basic divisions of sacred time: (1) the first division is found in the sanctuary itself, where there is a perpetual extension of sacred time; (2) the second division is found in the community around the sanctuary, where there is an intermittent extension of sacred time; (3) and the third division is found in the world outside the community, where there is no extension of sacred time.

As the priests work in the sanctuary on a daily basis, they are perpetually living in the domain of sacred time. As the laity only approach the sanctuary when they have an offering to bring, they are only occasionally living in the domain of sacred time. The Israelite measurement of time was based on the lunar calendar, consisting of a 7-day week and 12 lunar months. Within this annual calendar, they not only engaged in voluntary worship, but also observed numerous mandatory times for worship: (1) the Sabbath (i.e., weekly); (2) the New Moon (i.e., monthly); (3) the Seventh New Moon (every seventh month); (4) Passover and the Festival of Unleavened Bread (the spring barley-harvest); (5) the Festival of Pentecost (the summer wheat-harvest); (6) Yom Kippur and the Festival of Tabernacles (the autumn fruit-harvest); (7) the Sabbath Year (every seventh year the land was to rest from sowing); (8) and the Jubilee Year (every seven times seven years all people and lands were to be returned to their ancestral allotments).

A close examination of these sacred times will reveal that each of them enjoined the people to observe a mandatory period of rest, whereby each occasion may be understood as an extension of the meaning of the Sabbath. Thus, our understanding of sacred time is essentially tied to our understanding of the meaning of the Sabbath: a day of rest for the laity (Ex. 20:8-11), but a day of work for the priesthood (Num. 28:9-10). This oft-ignored contrast between the laity and the priesthood is important, for it points to the fact that man's rest from common work is not merely in order that he might be personally refreshed, but in order that he might express faithful dependence on the sacred work of the priesthood, and more especially on God. Recall that the sacred work of God consists in the establishing of the Kingdom of God: first encountered in creation, where he works to produce a sanctuary and then rests within it; and then encountered in the covenant, through which he works to restore that sanctuary in order that he might once more rest within it. Although from an earthly point of view, this work of restoration might remain incomplete, from a heavenly point of view it is completed from eternity, for it is held secure within the sovereign purpose of the Godhead. Thus, while the laity continues to do common work, they have nevertheless been chosen to serve as the instruments of this sacred work: by resting from the former, they bear witness to the latter, both that which has been accomplished, and that which has not yet been accomplished. In the Sabbath, Israel waits upon YHWH. And in her festal calendar, she also commemorates the work that he has already done on her behalf: the work of creation as resumed in the covenant (Sabbath, New Moon, and the Seventh New Month); the work of bringing Israel out of Egypt (Passover); the work of providing her with food (the festivals of Unleavened Bread, Pentecost, and Tabernacles); the work of providing atonement for her sins (Yom Kippur); the work of providing the land of Canaan (Sabbath Year); and the work of giving the people their portion within the land of Canaan (Jubilee).

In the New Testament, the divine work that was inaugurated in the covenant reaches its appointed fulfillment. Jesus' well-known practice of working on the day of rest is not so much a declaration of his freedom from some inconvenient ritual as it is a way of identifying his work with God's work: *So, because Jesus was doing these things on the Sabbath, the Jews persecuted him. Jesus said to them, "My Father is always at his work to this very day, and I too am working." For this reason the Jews tried all the harder to kill him; not only was he breaking the Sabbath, but he was even calling God his own Father, making himself equal with God* (John 5:16-18). Accordingly, Jesus calls himself the "Lord of the Sabbath," and, by extension, lord over all other sacred times (Matt. 12:8; Mk 2:28; Lk 6:5). Jesus' teaching implied that Sabbath observance was not only a commemoration of the work of the Father, but also a cryptic commemoration of the work of the Son. In the Gospel of John, for example, he makes it a special point to work not only on the Sabbath, but on every major festal day in the Israelite calendar (John 5:1, 6:3-4, 7:2, 10:22)! The culmination of Jesus' work is, of course, the Cross, and once more we are reminded that this too took place on the Jewish festival of Passover, and also that the birth of the church took place in the Jewish festival of Pentecost. Thus, from a Christian point of view, sacred times should not be regarded as empty rituals, but as meaningful expressions of faith which find their fulfillment in the work of Jesus Christ: all of the work that God the Father ever did is contained in the person of Jesus Christ. Accordingly, the dimension of sacred time does not simply disappear, but passes into the life of the believer, for wherever Christ is acknowledged, the Sabbath is implicitly observed, along with the festivals, the Passover, Yom Kippur, and the year of Jubilee. As with holy space, so with holy time: it extends through Christ to the community of believers.

Once the believer has become a sanctuary for the presence of God, once he has become a member of the holy priesthood, once he has been made to dwell in the dimension of sacred space and sacred time, he must guard ever more carefully the frontier between himself and the world. The fact that he dwells in sacred space enjoins upon his person the requirement that he be holy in all places, and the fact that he dwells in sacred time enjoins upon his work the requirement that he act in the capacity of a servant at all times. As a priest, he can no longer live a divided life, but the whole of his person and work must be permeated by holiness. Like the Levitical priesthood, he has no earthly inheritance, save that of the sanctuary, and he has no earthly work, save the work of the sanctuary. His life is a life of worship and service, albeit within the sanctuary of his own soul, and to such sanctuaries as exist within the souls of others. The challenge presented by the prospect of such a life is greater than any other. And yet, it is not a challenge we undertake out of fear, but out of a desire for deeper fellowship with God: it is deep calling to deep, creation's eager longing. In the chapters that follow, we shall attempt to examine this life in greater detail by inquiring into the nature of holiness and sin, and into the question of what it means to lead a life of worship in the presence of God.

PART II
THE DESTINY OF MAN
MADE POSSIBLE

CHAPTER ONE

The Holiness of God and the Sinfulness of Man

Be holy because I, YHWH your God, am holy.

Leviticus 19:2

In the previous chapter, I said that the spiritual life of worship consists in a series of acts, the most important of which was the deity's indwelling of the sanctuary. This initial act is what transforms a person's soul into a temple, invests them with their priestly vocation, and calls them to a life of separation from the world and separation to God.

Up to now, I have spoken very plainly about this event, but I have not said anything about how it occurs. And this of course is the primary point of interest, for we should like to know not only how it is possible for holiness to pass to sinful man without destroying him, but also how it is possible for this to become an event within us. In order to answer these questions, we shall have to take a much closer look at holiness and sin as they are expressed in the context of the sanctuary itself.

YHWH is holy. Man is a sinner. Therefore, if YHWH is to take up his abode within sinful man, and if man is to become a participant in the holiness of God, then this relationship can only ensue in the form of acts that negotiate between the realms of the holy and the sinful. In other words, this relationship does not happen as a matter of course, but has to be maintained and repaired. As we shall see, this is precisely what the acts performed in the sanctuary are intended to do: to maintain and repair the relationship between man and God.

The Holiness of God

Holiness is the principle attribute of God. God refers to the divine name "YHWH" as "the name of his holiness" (Lev. 20:3, 22:2). In this way, he uniquely identifies himself with his holiness, not because this attribute excludes all the others, but because this attribute permeates all the others with the distinctive mark of his divinity. In *The Idea of the Holy*, Rudolf Otto provides an excellent definition of holiness as the *mysterium tremendum*: the tremendous mystery, evocative of humility and of awe, reverence, and fascination, or what the scriptures refer to as the "fear of the Lord." By virtue of this mysterious quality, the being, goodness, and beauty of God, and all his other intelligible attributes, are retained and yet placed beyond the reach of man's natural comprehension.

Along with holiness, love and righteousness are the two attributes that the scripture most frequently ascribes to God. Now these are intelligible attributes to the extent that we already know something about them from our own experience. But when applied to God, they are permeated with holiness in such a way that, although they remain clearly intelligible, they are no longer fully comprehensible. Thus, when we say that God is loving, we are not only saying that he is gracious, but that his graciousness consists in the gift of his holiness. And when we say that God is righteous, we are not only saying that he is just, but that his justice consists in the faithfulness he exhibits toward his holiness. Consequently, God's manner of operation in the sanctuary is essentially an expression of these two attributes: in love, he gives the gift of his holy presence; and in righteousness, he exercises faithfulness to the holiness of his presence.

All of this finds concrete expression in the rules governing the care of the sanctuary. God is holy (Heb. *qodesh*). Beyond the sphere of holiness lies what we referred to in the previous chapter as the sphere of the "common" (Heb. *hol*). Now this common order of reality may stand in a relation of compatibility or non-compatibility with holiness: when it is compatible with holiness it is said to be "pure" (Heb. *tahor*); when it is not compatible with holiness is it said to be "impure" (Heb. *tame*). These then are the basic terms that govern the relationship between man and the divinity as it is lived out in the midst of the sanctuary. To fail to keep the boundaries of holiness is to risk desecration, in which one treats the holy as common, or defilement, in which one brings the holy into contact with that which is impure. Moreover, it is to endanger one's own life, since the deity's holiness manifests itself in the form of a consuming fire, purifying whatever it comes into contact with by destroying everything that is contrary to it: *For YHWH your God is a consuming fire, a jealous God* (Deut. 4:24). Accordingly, YHWH gives the following instruction to the priests: *"You must distinguish between the holy and the common, between the impure and the pure, and you must teach the Israelites all the decrees YHWH has given them through Moses* (Lev. 10:10-11).

God's Communication of Holiness

YHWH alone is holy, and therefore the origin of all holiness: *Who will not fear you, O Lord, and bring glory to your name? For you alone are holy* (Rev. 15:4).

But while YHWH is the origin of holiness, by virtue of his love he wills to communicate that holiness to the common order of space and time, physical objects, and people: *That you may know that I am YHWH who sanctifies you* (Ex. 31:13). Thus, he can transform an ordinary location into his holy sanctuary. He can transform an ordinary object into his holy property. And he can transform an ordinary person into his holy servant. The soul of man, for example, can be transformed at one and the same time into the sanctuary of God, the property of God, and the servant of God. In all of these cases, this transformation of the common into the holy is referred to as sanctification.

Now we may immediately observe that while sanctification is a simple matter when it involves objects, it is a more complicated matter when it involves people. In order for sanctification to be effected on a passive entity like an object, divine action alone is sufficient, and the resultant condition is called "ritual holiness." In order for sanctification to be effected on a passive-active entity like a person, divine action must meet with human cooperation, and the resultant condition is not only one of ritual holiness, but also one of "moral holiness." Accordingly, the Old Testament will refer to man's holiness in two ways: it will refer to his ritual holiness as a quality he already possesses by virtue of his belonging to YHWH: *For you are a holy people to YHWH your God. YHWH your God has chosen you out of all the peoples on the face of the earth to be his people, his treasured possession* (Deut. 7:6); But it will refer to his moral holiness as a quality he has yet to possess by virtue of his obedience to YHWH: *You are to be holy to me because I, YHWH, am holy, and I have set you apart from the nations to be my own* (Lev. 20:26). In the same way, the New Testament speaks of believers as saints, or "holy ones": *To the church of God in Corinth, together with all the saints throughout Achaia* (II Cor. 1:1); But it will then go on to say that they are called to be saints, or "holy ones": *To the church of God in Corinth; to those sanctified in Christ Jesus and called to be holy* (I Cor. 1:2). Having said that, it is crucial to bear in mind that the difference between ritual holiness and moral holiness is not that the former comes from God and the latter comes from man. On the contrary, holiness always comes from God—thus, when we speak of moral holiness we are not saying that man's obedience makes him holy, but we are saying that man's obedience brings him into greater communion with the one who makes him holy. As man draws near to God, God draws near to man (James 4:8).

On Ritual Holiness

By ritual holiness, we mean that space and time, an object, or a person has been set apart from the common order of reality as the special property of YHWH. This can happen in one of three ways: (1) first, by coming into direct contact with YHWH; (2) second, by entrance into a covenant with YHWH; (3) and third, whenever a member of that covenant dedicates something to YHWH.

The first of these three ways has already been encountered in our discussion about the divinity's indwelling of the sanctuary. When the divine presence descended upon Sinai, the mountain itself became holy (Ex. 19:23). When the divine presence moved from Sinai to the Tabernacle, the sanctuary became holy (Ex. 40:34-35). And when divine presence sent fire upon the sacrificial altar, it too became holy (Lev. 9:23-24). In turn, this quality of holiness was transferred to the sacrificial animals brought by the laity (Ex. 29:37), the sacrificial flesh eaten by the priests (Lev. 6:26), and the sacrificial remains that were dumped outside the camp (Lev. 4:11-12). All of these things came into direct contact with the divine presence. For persons, however, no such immediate process of sanctification was possible. Moses certainly expressed a desire for this, but his request was denied on the grounds that holiness would prove destructive to sinful man: *Then Moses said, "O let me behold your presence!"… But YHWH said, "You cannot see my face, for man may not see me and live"* (Ex. 33:18-20); *Fire came out from the presence of YHWH and consumed [Nadab and Abihu], and they died before YHWH* (Lev. 10:1-2); *Fire came out from YHWH and consumed the 250 men who were offering incense* (Num. 16:35).

In view of the danger posed by holiness to sinful man, the ritual sanctification of persons was established by entrance into a covenant with YHWH. In other words, the covenant is not only the means whereby the divinity gives himself to his people, but it is also the means whereby the divinity claims his people as his own. In the Bible, this covenant is formally established by means of a sacrificial ritual, part of which involves setting the participants apart as the property of YHWH. Nevertheless, from within the covenant itself, ritual holiness was further divided into different grades, reflective of the level of attachment each individual had to the sanctuary, the place from which holiness emanated. Therefore, the covenant instituted the use of a sacred anointing oil to serve as a sign of these different grades of holiness, beginning with the sanctuary itself (Ex. 30:22-29). The holiest individual in the community was the high priest, who had the anointing oil poured over his head (Lev. 8:12). Next in order of holiness were the lay priests, who had the anointing oil sprinkled on their bodies (Lev. 8:30). And next in order of holiness was the tribe of Levi, who were not anointed, but nevertheless ordained to serve as assistants to the priesthood (Num. 8:5-26). Still, notwithstanding the special holiness of the high priest, the lay priests, and the Levites, a general quality of holiness prevailed in the life of every individual Israelite.

As for the members of the covenant, they had the ability as well as the responsibility to sanctify their possessions by dedicating them to the service of the sanctuary. In some cases this was mandatory, as in the giving of tithes or festal offerings. But in other cases this was voluntary, as in the giving of one's material possessions, such as an animal, a house, or a field (Lev. 27:1-34), or in the giving of oneself to a period of service, such as we find in the Nazirite Vow (Num. 6:1-21). Sometimes these acts were temporary, meaning that an individual could redeem whatever they dedicated at a later date. But oftentimes these acts were permanent, meaning that the individual could not redeem what they dedicated, but that it remained forever the property of YHWH. The Nazirite vow, for example, could be taken on a temporary basis, as in the case of the Apostle Paul (Acts 18:18). But it could also be taken on a permanent basis, as in the case of Samuel (I Sam. 1:11), Sampson (Jdg. 13:5), or John the Baptist (Luke 1:15). In every such case, however, the rationale was always the same: namely, for the quality of holiness to radiate out from the sanctuary to the priesthood to the laity in ever increasing measure until it should saturate the whole nation of Israel.

On Moral Holiness

Now we come to moral holiness. When YHWH sets man apart, he takes ownership of him, but that doesn't necessarily mean that he and man are in perfect communion with one another. In order for there to be perfect communion between the two, their wills must be in agreement with one another, which is to say that the will of man must be brought into conformity with the will of God. True, man is already holy in the sense of his having been adopted by God, but he is not yet holy in the sense of his living in obedience to God.

What does this mean in practical terms? In ancient Israel, it meant the fear of YHWH expressed in faithfulness to the covenant of YHWH: *Fear YHWH your God, serve him only and take your oaths in his name. Do not follow other gods, the gods of the peoples around you* (Deut. 6:13-14). As we have seen, this covenant consisted in a promise of blessing, and in commands that were to be obeyed. To be faithful, then, meant to trust in the promise of God, and to be obedient to the commands of God. In trust, Israel depended upon YHWH's love and righteousness to perfect their life of communion together. In obedience, Israel imitated YHWH's love and righteousness in order that she might enter more fully into that life of communion. As YHWH had given himself and showed himself holy, so she should give herself in humility, and awe, reverence, and love before his holiness. Thus, while we may enumerate a multiplicity of commandments, all of them can be summed up in the twofold duty to love one's neighbor man and to love one's God: *Love your neighbor as yourself, I am YHWH* (Lev. 19:18); *Love YHWH your God with all your heart and with all your soul and with all your strength* (Deut. 6:5). Indeed, this twofold duty can be further condensed into a single duty, for one's duty to man is included in one's duty to God inasmuch as man made in the image of God is the property of God: *YHWH said to*

Moses, "Say to the Israelites: 'When a man or woman wrongs another in any way and so is unfaithful to YHWH, that person is guilty and must confess the sin he has committed (Num. 5:5-7).

All of this points to the fact that a man may be ritually holy, and yet fail to be morally holy. He may be set apart as the property of YHWH, but his will may still be in rebellion against the will of YHWH. Like a rebellious son, there is a sense in which he belongs to his father, and a sense in which he does not belong to his father. He has been adopted as a son, but he does not yet live a life worthy of the sonship he has received: *Hear, O heavens! Listen, O earth! For YHWH has spoken: "I reared children and brought them up, but they have rebelled against me. The ox knows his master, the donkey his owner's manger, but Israel does not know, my people do not understand* (Is. 1:2-3). By the same token, however, as he grows in steadfast trust and obedience, in just such proportion does he grow in the blessedness of his communion with God: in trust, he shows his dependence upon the love and righteousness of God; in obedience, he brings his own life into consonance with that same love and righteousness: *Trust in YHWH with all your heart and lean not on your own understanding; in all your ways acknowledge him, and he will make your paths straight* (Prov. 3:5-6). Thus, the larger task of being faithful to the covenant of God, while clearly of service to the cause of social justice, is ultimately about a faith and obedience that brings man into the joy of deeper communion with God: *Blessed are they whose ways are blameless, who walk according to the Torah of YHWH... My soul is consumed with longing for your laws at all times... Direct me in the path of your commands, for there I find delight... You are my portion, O YHWH; I have promised to obey your words* (Ps. 119:1, 20, 35, 57). Here, we arrive back where we started: man was created in order that he might bring glory to God, which is to say that he might worship God, which is to say that he might know him, serve him, and enjoy him forever. To be sure, this is not a task that man has the power to accomplish on his own, but it is nevertheless the task for which he has been set apart. The sanctification of man culminates in the cultivation of moral holiness.

The Sin and Impurity of Man

Sin is the opposite of holiness. In the first place, it is an act of rebellion against the kingship of God, whereby man withdraws himself from communion with God. In the second place, it is the resulting condition of man's alienation from God, a condition the scriptures describe as a kind of living death: *You must not eat from the tree of the knowledge of good and evil, for on the day you eat of it, you shall dying die* (Gen. 2:17). Here again, we may recall the words of Jeremiah: *Blessed is the one who trusts in YHWH, whose trust alone is YHWH. He shall be like a tree planted by waters, that sends out its roots by a stream* (Jer. 17:7-8); *Cursed is the one who trusts in man, who depends on flesh for his strength and turns his thoughts from YHWH. He will be like a bush in the desert; he will not see prosperity when it comes* (Jer. 17:5-6).

When man sins, the whole person is rendered a sinner, which is another way of saying that the whole person is rendered "godless." Here again, the word "sin" not only signifies a transient act, but also a persistent condition, for when man transgresses the command of God, he at the same time crosses over from a godly existence to a godless existence. In the crossing of this threshold, man goes from a condition of innocence, in which he knows only God, to a condition of guilt in which he knows godliness and godlessness in contradistinction from one another: he acquires the "knowledge of good and evil." And so, not only has he performed a godless act, not only is he in a condition of godlessness, but he has been rendered unable to go back to the way he was before. For man to say that he is innocent is a lie; for man to suppose he can once more become innocent is naïve; therefore, the solution to the problem of sin is not a journey backward into innocence, but a journey forward into redemption.

According to this view, man is not as our western sages insist a social creature, but as our eastern sages insist a religious creature. To call man a sinner is not to say that he is socially dysfunctional, but that he godless, and therefore worldly. For this reason, the gravity of sin has less to do with whatever consequences it may have in the social sphere, as for example how much damage it does to others, and more to do with the fact that it disregards the lordship of God—indeed, it betrays a preference to live without the lordship of God. Ultimately, the more godless man becomes, the more he will forget his religious vocation altogether, and the more he will come to define his own goodness in terms of social cooperation. He will perceive himself as good by virtue of the fact that he cooperates with his fellow man, but will fail to see that such cooperation is mutiny against the holiness of God. Their fellowship is the fellowship of pirates, who have agreed to plunder the world and overthrow its divine captain. Thus, the concept of sin carries with it not only the idea of man's transgression, his removal from the divine presence, and his inability to return, but also the idea of his corruption: as man in his innocence knew nothing of godlessness, so man in his corruption knows nothing of God. *For although they knew God, they neither glorified him as God nor gave thanks to him, but their thinking became futile and their foolish hearts were darkened* (Rom. 1:21).

Sinful Man's Communication of Impurity

As mentioned, the sinful condition is a kind of living death. When man withdraws himself from communion with God, he not only separates himself from God's holiness, but he also separates himself from the sustaining power of the divinity's being, goodness, and beauty. He is like a branch that has been cut off from the vine: while in the strictest sense of the word the branch continues to exist, it is nevertheless dead, and therefore in a process of decay. In biblical terms, this condition of death is called "sin," and this process of decay is called "impurity." As God is the origin of holiness, so sinful man is the origin of impurity.

Now decay is a process that communicates itself to the surrounding environment. And so, just as God has the ability to communicate his holiness to others, sinful man can communicate his impurity to the common order of space and time, objects, and other persons. Sinful man is essentially a carrier of impurity: he can transform an ordinary place into an impure place; he can transform an ordinary object into an impure object; and he can transform an ordinary person into an impure person. In all of these cases, this transformation of the common into the impure is referred to as defilement (the opposite of sanctification).

As with sanctification, there are two different kinds of defilement, corresponding to the passive and active aspects of mankind's existence. As a passive creature, man's being, un-sustained by divinity's life, sinks back into its own native mortality, and this becomes the source of what is called "ritual impurity." As an active creature, man's goodness, un-sustained by the divinity's ways, sinks back into its own native futility, avarice, and wickedness, and these become the source of what is called "moral impurity." Interestingly, these are the very problems Qoheleth seeks to address in the book of Ecclesiastes. Apart from the divine presence, man cannot fulfill his divinely ordained purpose of living in communion with God. On the one hand, he retains an obscure knowledge of this purpose: *[God] has set eternity in the hearts of men; yet they cannot fathom what God has done from beginning to end* (Ecc. 3:11). But on the other hand, he cannot actualize this purpose, whereby his sense of purpose is condemned to express itself in an endless striving that is cut short only on the day of his death: *So I hated life, because the work that is done under the sun was grievous to me. All of it is meaningless, a chasing after the wind. I hated all the things I had toiled for under the sun, because I must leave them to one who comes after me. And who knows whether he will be a wise man or a fool? Yet he will have control over all the work into which I have poured my effort and skill under the sun. This too is meaningless* (Ecc. 2:17-19). In the end, man's mortality combined with the futility of his labor leads to avarice, and avarice leads to wickedness. *And I saw something else under the sun: in the place of justice, there was wickedness; in the place of righteousness, there was wickedness* (Eccl. 3:16).

On Ritual Impurity

When we say that a man is ritually impure, we are saying that he is in a state contrary to that of holiness, not by virtue of any individual act, but by virtue of his own mortality. In other words, this kind of impurity is generated passively by the natural processes of his bodily life, such as the depletion of his vitality, the decay of his flesh, and the extinction of his life.

In the Bible, there are three causes of this kind of impurity, corresponding to the three stages in mortality just mentioned: (1) discharges of sexual fluids (Lev. 12 and 15); (2) the degeneration of the skin (Lev. 13-14); (3) and the human corpse (Num. 19): *YHWH said to Moses, "Command the Israelites to send away from the camp anyone who has an infectious skin disease, or a discharge of any kind, or who is ritually impure because of a dead body. Send away male and female alike; send them outside the camp, where I dwell among them* (Num. 5:1-3).

Again, these three causes of impurity are all part of the natural processes of bodily life. For this reason, they are devoid of moral significance, but they are not on that account devoid of ritual significance. For example, a man or a woman who has come into contact with a corpse has not become morally guilty, but they have become unfit to enter the sanctuary: they are tainted by the residue of mortality and must therefore remain outside the domain of the immortal God. Thus, the practical significance of ritual impurity is that it renders the individual unfit to enter the sanctuary, whereas the theoretical significance of ritual impurity is that it signifies man's sinful condition. As a creature made for union with God, man's mortality is made to depend upon the life of the divinity. Thus, when his mortality is no longer dependent upon the life of the divinity, it becomes a sign of his alienation from God. For this reason, man's mortality appears in a different light than that of the cell, the plant, or the animal: it is not a part of the natural cycle degeneration and regeneration, but it is in the strictest sense of the word death. Indeed, it is by virtue of man's spiritual death that death enters into creation with the acquired sense of infinite loss that renders it a source of dread: *There is hope for a tree: if it is cut down, it will sprout again, and its shoots will not fail… But man dies and is laid low; he breathes his last and is no more* (Job 14:7-10).

The primary agent of ritual purification is water. The procedure for ritual purification is threefold: (1) to terminate contact with the source of one's impurity; (2) to wash with water; (3) and to observe a mandatory waiting period. This process of ritual purification was necessary for anyone who wished to approach the sanctuary for worship. Failure to purify oneself was to risk one's own life and to commit sacrilege against God: *You must keep the Israelites separate from the things that make them impure, so they will not die in their impurity for defiling my dwelling place, which is among them* (Lev. 15:31). Care to purify oneself, however, was to respect the boundary between sin and holiness, to humble oneself in one's sin and to stand in fear before the holiness of God, just as the people had done in their first encounter with YHWH at Sinai: *YHWH said to Moses, "I am going to come to you in a dense cloud… Go to the people and warn them to stay pure today and tomorrow: have them wash their clothes… Put limits for the people around the mountain and tell them 'Be careful that you do no go up to the mountain or touch the foot of it. Whoever touches the mountain shall surely be put to death'"* (Ex. 19:9-12); *When the people saw the thunder and lightning and heard the trumpet and saw the mountain in smoke, they trembled with fear and stood at a distance and said to Moses, "Speak to us yourself and we will listen. But do not have God speak to us or we will die"* (Ex. 20:18-19).

On Moral Impurity

When we say that a man is morally impure, we are saying that he is in a state contrary to that of holiness, not by virtue of his mortality, but by virtue of his individual acts. In other words, this kind of impurity is generated actively by man's wickedness, not only against his fellow man, but first and foremost against his God.

Although all sinful acts cause moral impurity, the three that are the greatest sources of impurity are idolatry, murder, and sexual licentiousness. However, the reason why these three sins are graver than others is not because of their impact on the social sphere, but because of their impact on the religious sphere. From a biblical point of view, man's moral vocation consists in his relationship with God, and this provides the rational basis for the three prohibitions we have just mentioned: (1) The gravest sin of which man is capable is the sin of idolatry, for this consists essentially in a love of the world and a hatred toward God (Ex. 20:5-6); (2) The next highest sin of which man is capable is murder, not only because it is an attack upon one's neighbor, but especially because it is an attack upon God. Among all living creatures, man alone is made in the image of God, meaning that he alone serves as the icon of the deity in the sanctuary of the created order. Viewed in this light, murder amounts to an act of sacrilege, and specifically the one known as iconoclasm (Gen. 9:6). (3) The next highest sin of which man is capable is that of sexual licentiousness, which again is not only an act against one's neighbor, but especially an act against God. Man is the icon of the deity, and his sexuality is the tie that binds his individual life into that organic form of life we call "family," whereby sexual activity can result in either a reflection or a distortion of the divine image. Thus, whereas murder commits sacrilege by destroying the icon of the deity, sexual licentiousness commits sacrilege by either desecrating or profaning the icon of the deity. To desecrate the divine image is to mar, deface, or disfigure it (as in incest, homosexuality, and bestiality). To profane the divine image is to treat it as though it were common property, whether non-consensually (as in seduction, molestation, and rape) or consensually (as in adultery, fornication, and prostitution).

What does moral impurity do? First it defiles the sanctuary:

In this way [the high priest] will make atonement for the Most Holy Place because of the impurity and rebellion of the Israelites, whatever their sins have been (Lev. 16:16). Second, it provokes the wrath of God: *[The priests] are to be responsible for the care of the sanctuary and the altar, so that wrath will not fall on the Israelites again* (Num. 18:5). And third, it renders the life of the sinner forfeit: *From now on the Israelites must not go near to the Tent of Meeting, or they will bear the consequences of their sin and will die* (Num. 18:22). For grave sins, such as idolatry, murder, and sexual licentiousness, impurity is not only communicated to the sanctuary, but also to the land itself: *For all these things were done by the people who lived in the land before you, and the land became defiled* (Lev. 18:27). Thus, the accumulation of impurity presents a twofold danger: first, that the deity will be forced to vacate the sanctuary; and second, that the land will vomit out its people. Indeed, this is precisely what happened in ancient Israel: as a result of the impurity accumulated in the sanctuary, YHWH was forced to vacate the sanctuary: *Then the glory of YHWH departed from over the threshold of the temple and stopped above the cherubim. While I watched, the cherubim spread their wings and rose from the ground, and as they went, the wheels went with them* (Ezek. 10:18-19); and as a result of the impurity accumulated in the land, Israel was invaded by foreigners and exiled from her homeland in a series of deportations: *So YHWH was very angry with Israel and removed them from his presence* (II Kgs. 17:18); *It was because of YHWH's anger that all this happened to Jerusalem and Judah, and in the end he thrust them from his presence* (II Kgs. 24:20).

As the remedy for ritual impurity was living water, so the remedy for moral impurity is sacrificial blood. This sacrificial blood achieves three things, corresponding to the three primary effects of moral impurity: (1) first, the application of the blood to the sanctuary purifies it from its defilement; (2) second, the purification of the sanctuary propitiates the divine wrath; (3) and third, by propitiating the divine wrath, the life of the animal effectually serves as a ransom for the life of the sinner. In summary, the water and the blood work together to purify man from his sin. And in turn, man's participation in the covenant and his faithful trust and obedience work together to sanctify him and make him holy. These are the acts that negotiate between the realms of the holy and the sinful, maintaining and repairing the relationship between man and God. Nevertheless, YHWH still remains the origin, criterion, and giver of holiness. It is by his grace that the work of sanctification has been initiated, and it is only by his grace that the work of sanctification can be brought to completion.

CHAPTER TWO

The Ministry of Ritual Ablution

YHWH said to Moses, "Go to the people and warn them to stay pure today and tomorrow: let them wash their clothes."

Exodus 19:10

Like a tree watered by a stream, man's life is sustained by his relationship with God, and sin is an act of rebellion that severs that relationship. Once performed, it renders the whole man a sinner, whereby he transmits the quality of sinfulness to the world around him in the form of impurity. In turn, this impurity is communicated both passively through his mortal body (called ritual impurity) and actively through his wicked deeds (called moral impurity).

Now if the act of sin removes man from the divine presence, then the fact of impurity prevents him from re-entering the divine presence a second time. Thus, even before an individual can approach the deity, he must be first be washed of his ritual impurity. By undergoing this initial rite of ablution, by purifying himself with water, man humbles himself in his sin, and stands in fear before the holiness of God: *Guard your steps when you go to the house of God* (Eccl. 5:1).

But while man's act of worship begins in humility and fear,

this is only the first step in his relationship with God. In his righteousness, the deity remains faithful to his holiness, and therefore adamant in his rejection of impurity. But in his love, the deity desires to communicate his holiness to man, and therefore provides him with the means of purification. Thus, the requirement of ritual purification reflects the deity's justice, but also the deity's grace, for it both condemns and removes impurity. By extension, the whole work of the sanctuary is captured in the concept of grace, for it is by grace that man is brought near to God, it is by grace that his relationship with God is maintained and repaired, and it is by grace that he is educated from the fear of God to the god-fearing love of God: *And now, O Israel, what does YHWH your God ask of you but to fear YHWH your God, to walk in all his ways, to love YHWH your God, to serve him with all your heart and with all your soul, keeping YHWH's commandments and laws, which I enjoy upon you today, for your own good* (Deut. 10:12-13).

Moses' Ministry of Ritual Ablution (Lev. 12-15)

In the Bible, ritual impurity is expressed in three different forms: the depletion of man's vitality, the decay of his flesh, and the extinction of his life. This threefold classification is not arbitrary, but has its basis in the creational blessing of offspring, food, and the breath of life.

God's life is immortal, but man's life is mortal, and this mortal condition produces a residue that renders him unfit to enter into the divine presence. As man is born into impurity, he cannot really feel any guilt over it: *How can one born of a woman be pure?* (Job 25:4b). Nevertheless, if he wishes to enter into the presence of the deity, he must be willing to purify himself: *If a person who is impure does not purify himself, he must be cut off from the community because he has defiled the sanctuary of YHWH* (Num. 19:20).

For this reason, the ministry of ritual ablution is central to the work of Moses as well as to the work of Jesus Christ. It is the first step in the process of bringing sinful man near to the holiness of God: *On the day you were born your cord was not cut, nor were you washed with water to make you clean... I bathed you with water and washed the blood from you and anointed you with oil* (Ezek. 16:4-9); *Christ loved the church by giving himself up for her, to make her holy, having purified her by the washing of water through the word* (Eph. 5:25-26).

The Causes of Ritual Impurity

As mentioned in the previous chapter, the causes of ritual impurity are three: (1) discharges of sexual fluids (Lev. 12 and 15); (2) the degeneration of the skin (Lev. 13-14); (3) and the human corpse (Num. 19): *YHWH said to Moses, "Command the Israelites to send away from the camp anyone who has an infectious skin disease, or a discharge of any kind, or who is ritually impure because of a dead body. Send away male and female alike; send them outside the camp, where I dwell among them* (Num. 5:1-3).

In the Bible's discussion of ritual impurity resulting from the discharge of sexual fluids, the primary causes are childbirth, menses, and semen. In the Bible's discussion of impurity resulting from the degeneration of the skin, the primary cause is a condition denoted by the word "tzara'at," often taken to refer to leprosy, but having a much broader valence of meaning that not only includes a wide variety of degenerative conditions affecting man's body, but also a wide variety of degenerative conditions affecting man's works, such as fabrics, building materials, and so forth. In the Bible's discussion of impurity resulting from the human corpse, the primary cause is of course death itself. The corpse itself is permanently impure, and anyone who has come into contact with the corpse, or been in the same room with a corpse, or even steps on the grave of a corpse immediately contracts its impurity. The corpse is, therefore, the ultimate source of ritual impurity, and the one in which all others find their fundamental basis.

A careful examination of the scriptures will reveal that all these impurities fall into one of two different levels of intensity: some of them are minor, and some of them are major. Minor impurities are marked by the fact that they generally take less time to purify and do not cause defilement to the sanctuary (i.e., they do not require that the individual bring a sacrificial offering). Major impurities are marked by the fact that they generally take longer to purify and do cause defilement to the sanctuary (i.e., they do require that the individual bring a sacrificial offering). Now of the major impurities, the most severe are those in which the source of impurity cannot be stopped, meaning that they cannot be purified, and that the individual so afflicted cannot approach the sanctuary for worship. In order of intensity, they include: (1) the dead corpse (not to be confused with the person who contracts impurity by coming into contact with a dead corpse); (2) the person suffering from a perpetual state of bodily decay (e.g., leprosy); (3) and the person suffering from a perpetual discharge of sexual fluid (e.g., gonorrhea or chronic bleeding).

The Process of Ritual Purification

As mentioned, the agent of ritual purification is water. In particular, the ancients exhibited a preference for what was called "living water" (i.e., running water). This preference for living water can be explained by virtue of the fact that still water is capable of contracting impurity (Lev. 11:34-35), whereas living water is not (Lev. 11:36). Rivers were widely regarded as providing the best source of living waters, since they not only washed away impurity, but they carried the impurity downstream. Accordingly, sanctuaries were often located near rivers: for example, the Garden of Eden, the Jerusalem temple, and Ezekiel's vision of the third temple.

Before approaching the sanctuary, a threefold process for ritual purification is required for the laity: (1) to terminate contact with the source of impurity; (2) to wash with water; (3) and to observe a waiting period of 1, 7, or more days (depending on the severity of the impurity). In principle, anyone can be purified as long as the source of their impurity is terminable; the only time a person cannot be purified is when the source of their impurity is interminable (e.g., death, leprosy, and chronic discharges). Likewise, physical objects that become impure can be purified, except in a few small cases: redeemable objects include wood, cloth, hide, metals (washed with water and impure for a day); and non-redeemable objects include pottery, moldy objects, carcasses (disposed of in an "impure place" [Lev. 14:40-41]).

Once inside the sanctuary, an additional process of ritual purification was required for the priesthood: *Aaron and his sons are to wash their hands and feet with water from [the laver]. Whenever they enter the Tent of Meeting, they shall wash with water so that they will not die. Also, when they approach the altar to minister by presenting an offering made to YHWH by fire, they shall wash their hands and feet so that they will not die* (Ex. 30:19-21). Here again, we find the greater one's proximity to the divine presence, the greater the requirements placed on purity, as well as on the avoidance of impurity. For example, whereas a layperson was required to purify himself from having come into contact with a corpse, a priest was forbidden to even have contact with a corpse (cf. Lev. 21:1-4 and 21:10-12). Again, whereas a layperson was required to purify himself from degenerative conditions of the flesh, a priest was forbidden to serve if he had any kind of bodily defect (Lev. 21:16-23). And again, whereas a layperson was required to purify himself after normal conjugal relations, a priest was forbidden to have normal conjugal relations with a woman who had been a prostitute, divorced, or widowed (cf. Lev. 21:7-8 and 21:13-15). In all of these requirements, the concern was the same: to humble oneself in one's sin and impurity and stand in fear before the holiness of YHWH. And yet, this was but a prelude to an even greater concern: namely, to take up his gracious and mysterious invitation to approach.

Jesus' Ministry of Ritual Ablution

Jesus' ministry does not set aside the problem of ritual impurity, but takes it up. The rite of purification was not simply an ancient convention that could quietly be set aside, but a real requirement arising out of the fact of man's sinfulness and the fact of the deity's holiness. To ignore it was to risk driving the deity out of his sanctuary and to invite destruction upon oneself and the whole community.

Moses provided water for purification so that man might have occasional access to the sanctuary of God. But Jesus provided in himself a spring of living water for purification so that man might have continual access to the sanctuary of God. Because his work consisted in transforming the soul into a sanctuary for the divine presence, it was therefore necessary for him to produce within man the highest possible level of ritual purity.

And thus, Jesus' work does not merely consist in washing man of his mortal residue, but in curing him of his mortal condition. Jesus not only brings man more fully into the divine presence, but at the same time answers once and for all the mysterious question of man's eternal destiny. For the Old Testament provides no clear instruction about the meaning of human mortality: *All go to the same place; all come from dust, and to dust all return. Who knows if the spirit of man rises upward and if the spirit of the animal goes down into the earth?* (Eccl. 3:21). But the New Testament proclaims the resurrection of the body: *And if the Spirit of him who raised Jesus from the dead is living in you, he who raised Christ from the dead will also give life to your mortal bodies through the Spirit who lives in you* (Rom. 8:11).

Jesus' Healing of the Ritually Impure

The fact that Jesus' ministry addressed the problem of ritual purification is not widely recognized. In the gospels, however, many of the miracles he performs are specifically directed toward individuals whose afflictions render them ritually impure, and therefore unable to approach the sanctuary of God.

In Jesus' ministry, he addresses the problem of ritual impurity in all three of its three classical forms, as in his healing of the woman with chronic bleeding, his healing of those with leprosy, and his raising of people from the dead. In all three of the synoptic gospels, this ministry to the ritually impure begins with the story of the healing of the leper: *When he came down from the mountainside, large crowds followed him. A man with leprosy came and knelt before him and said, "Lord, if you are willing, you can make me pure." Jesus reached out his hand and touched the man. "I am willing," he said. "Be pure!" Immediately he was cured of his leprosy. Then Jesus said to him, "See that you don't tell anyone. But go, show yourself to the priest and offer the gift Moses commanded, as a testimony to them* (Matt. 8:1-4; cf. Mk 1:40-45 and Lk. 5:12-15).

According to the Torah, Jesus' contact with the leper would have rendered him ritually impure. Moreover, while unintentional contraction of impurity was tolerated, intentional contraction of impurity was regarded as a serious offense. This raises the question of Jesus' attitude toward Moses: was his behavior consistent with the requirements of the Torah? Here, the answer is clearly "Yes": Jesus is not involved in contracting ritual impurity, but in healing ritual impurity. Indeed, he instructs the one healed to go to the temple, to show himself to the priest, and to offer a sacrificial gift, all in accordance with the requirements of the Torah. Of particular importance is his statement that all of this be done as a testimony to those serving at the temple. This is but an extension of his teaching in the Sermon on the Mount: *Do not think that I have come to abolish the Torah or the Prophets. I have not come to abolish them but to fulfill them. I tell you the truth, until heaven and earth disappear, not the smallest letter, not the least stroke of a pen, will by any means disappear from the Torah until everything is accomplished. Anyone who breaks one of the least of the these commandments and teaches others to do the same will be called least in the Kingdom of God. But whoever practices and teaches these commands will be called great in the Kingdom of God* (Matt. 5:17-19).

Thus, Jesus does not abolish the requirements of the Torah. On the contrary, he is the only one in whom both its minimal and maximal requirements are fully met. He meets its minimal requirements in that he does not defile himself by coming into contact with impurity. But he meets its maximal requirements in that he purifies the man and renders him fit to re-enter the sanctuary. For the Torah does not only require that man avoid ritual and moral impurity, but that he enter into a life of holiness through communion with God. Accordingly, Paul maintains that the Torah's requirements are eternally binding: *So then, the Torah is holy, and the commandment is holy, righteous, and good* (Rom. 7:12). Therefore the gospel cannot be said to consist in the abolition of these requirements, but rather in the proclamation that they have been met in the Messiah of Israel: *What the Torah was powerless to do in that it was weakened by the sinful nature, God did by sending his own Son in the likeness of sinful man to be a sin offering. And so he condemned sin in sinful man, in order that the righteous requirements of the Torah might be fully met in us* (Rom. 8:3-4). And the requirement that concerns us here is this, that man be cleansed from the stain of his mortal condition and brought near to the dwelling of the immortal God: *Let us draw near to God with a sincere heart in full assurance of faith, having our hearts sprinkled to cleanse us from a guilty conscience, and having our bodies washed with pure water* (Heb. 10:22).

Jesus the Stream of Living Water

Jesus' ministry during his lifetime consisted of signs pointing to the meaning of his ministry during Holy Week: what he accomplished for a few individuals while he walked the earth, he would accomplish for all individuals through his death and resurrection: a single act of purification that would provide a way for man to stand in the divine presence forever. His sacrifice brought not only blood (for moral purification), but also water (for ritual purification): *One of the soldiers pierced Jesus' side with a spear, bringing a sudden flow of blood and water. The man who saw it has given testimony, and his testimony is true* (John 19:34-35).

In John, the emphasis on blood is always accompanied by an emphasis on water. Indeed, the first miracle he records involves the famous story of the changing of water into wine. In this story, the text indicates that the water jars in question were used for the purposes of ritual purification (John 2:6), but that their contents were subsequently transformed into wine to be used in the celebration of a wedding banquet (John 2:9). In this way, the role of the water was transformed, so that it did not merely wash man from the outside, but became a source of nourishment to him from the inside. In Jesus, man is not only to be cleansed from the residue of mortality, but to be fed from the stream that waters the tree of the fruit of life. Thus, he brings forth a harvest of new wine, a sign marking the messianic age, the advent of the Kingdom of God: *"The days are coming," declares YHWH, "when the reaper will be overtaken by the plowman and the planter by the one treading grapes. New wine will drip from the mountains and flow from all the hills. I will restore my people Israel: they will rebuild ruined cities and inhabit them; they will plant vineyards and drink their wine; they will make gardens and eat their fruit. I will plant Israel in their own land, never again to be uprooted from the land I have given them," says YHWH your God* (Amos 9:13-15).

In John's gospel, the stream of living water that revitalizes man is no vague metaphor, but is explicitly identified with the gift of the Spirit. Although Jesus was well aware that ritual impurity could be contracted from outward things, he nevertheless insisted upon tracing it to its inward origin. And thus, while an outward washing with water was sufficient to treat the symptoms of ritual impurity, only an inward planting of the soul in the stream of life was sufficient to cure the ultimate cause of that ritual impurity. In speaking of the stream of life, he was speaking about the indwelling of the divine presence, through which mortal man would at last be brought back into union with the immortal

God. To Nicodemus, he says: *I tell you the truth, no one can enter the Kingdom of God unless he is born of water and the Spirit* (John 3:5); to the Samaritan woman, he says: *Everyone who drinks this water will be thirsty again, but whoever drinks the water I give him will never thirst. Indeed, the water I give him will become a spring of water welling up to eternal life* (John 4:10-14); and to the assembly of Israel, he says: *If anyone is thirsty, let him come to me and drink. Whoever believes in me, as the scripture has said, streams of living water will flow from within him." By this he meant the Spirit, whom those who believed in him were later to receive* (John 7:37-39).

Ultimately, then, Jesus' ministry of ritual purification points beyond itself to the gift of forgiveness and the gift of the Holy Spirit. His disciples are not outwardly washed in order that they might approach the deity's sanctuary, but they are inwardly revived by the abiding presence of the deity within the sanctuary of their own soul. To be sure, this may appear at first glance to be an impossibility, inasmuch as we have already stated that the holiness of the deity is lethal to sinful man. But this is really only to point out the necessity of the death and resurrection of Christ. For by virtue of his blood, man is made fit for the divine presence, and by virtue of his resurrected body, man is granted access to that same divine presence. And thus, in the midst of his mortality, man is joined with the life immortal: *But we have this treasure in jars of clay to show that this all-surpassing power is from God and not from us… Though outwardly we are wasting away, yet inwardly we are being renewed day by day* (II Cor. 4:7-18). Accordingly, the humility and fear which man owes to the deity is not expressed by his repeatedly washing himself with water, but by his repeatedly drinking from the fountain of life that is in Jesus Christ: *So then, just as you have received Christ Jesus as Lord, continue to live in him, rooted and built up in him, strengthened in the faith as your were taught, and overflowing with thankfulness* (Col. 2:6-7).

CHAPTER THREE

The Ministry of Sacrificial Atonement

*For the life of the flesh is in the blood, and I have given it
to you to make atonement for your lives on the altar.*

Leviticus 17:11

In the ministry of ritual ablution, man is washed in order that
he might be made fit to approach the sanctuary of the deity's
presence. Once inside the sanctuary, however, the relationship
between man and the deity is expressed through the act of
sacrificial worship, not only on the irregular occasions chosen by
man, but also on regular occasions chosen by the deity.

Sacrifice was universally recognized as the primary form of
religious worship in the ancient world. Nevertheless, not every
culture held the same views about its aims and methods, and it
is probable that many who participated in it did so largely on the
basis of convention. In the Bible, the deity takes up sacrifice as his
primary means of redemption. As such, its function is threefold: to
establish, maintain, and repair the relationship between YHWH
and Israel.

In the preceding chapters, we have already encountered the
sacrificial procedures whereby the covenant is established. In the
present chapter, we are concerned with the sacrificial procedure

whereby it is repaired. As a sinner, man is estranged from the deity not only on account of his mortal condition, but also on account of his moral failure. This results first and foremost in the forfeiture of his life, but can also result in the desecration of the deity's property, and in the defilement of the deity's sanctuary. Accordingly, remedial measures begin with the provision of ransom for the life of the sinner, but may also be extended to include reparation of the deity's property, and purification for the deity's sanctuary. All of these measures are expressions of a single idea, designated by the ancient word *kipper*, and usually translated "atonement" (at-one-ment).

Moses' Ministry of Sacrificial Atonement

As mentioned, the living creature stands at a point of intersection between the realms of the earthly and the divine. For this reason, the act of slaughter is not merely a physical act, but a metaphysical act, for it returns the body of the creature to the ground and it returns the life of the creature to the Creator: *the dust returns to the ground it came from, and the spirit returns to God who gave it* (Eccl. 12:7).

For ritual purposes, the life of the creature is signified by the blood, thus enabling it to be physically handled. A careful examination of how the blood is handled reveals that it is either poured out on the ground or applied in various ways to the sanctuary. In the latter case, the priest's behavior indicates that the sacrifice is meant to effect atonement: it is the blood that effects atonement by providing ransom for the life of the sinner: *For the life of the flesh is in the blood, and I have given it to you to make atonement for your lives on the altar* (Lev. 17:11).

As for the body of the creature, the inedible parts are disposed of in a pure place, and the edible parts are distributed as food between the altar, the priests and the laity. The manner in which this food is distributed bestows upon the act of slaughter one of three different levels of holiness: (1) most holy, in which the meat is given to the sanctuary; (2) holy, in which the meat is shared between the sanctuary and the laity; (3) and common, in which the meat is retained by the layperson, as in the hunting of wild game or the slaughter of domestic stock. All of the sacrifices dealt with in this chapter are most holy: their primary purpose is not to provide flesh for food, but to provide blood for atonement. Accordingly, the flesh is given to the sanctuary, and the blood is used to make ransom, reparation, or purification.

The Three Sacrifices for Atonement

There are three sacrifices for atonement that a person may bring on irregular occasions: the *Olah*, the *Asham*, and the *Hattat*. As we shall see, all of these sacrifices seek to repair the relationship between man and the deity by providing ransom for the life of the sinner, but the latter two also seek to address the repercussions of his sin by providing reparation for the deity's property and purification for the deity's sanctuary.

The *Olah* is usually translated simply as "Burnt Offering." Of the atoning sacrifices just mentioned, it is by far the most ancient, being the only one that is voluntary, and pre-dating the institution of the sanctuary. According to the scripture, its traditional function was to provide atonement for man's sin in the most generic sense, from the inner condition of his heart, to the things that he had done, to the things that he had left undone. The name of the offering means "going up," and is reflected in the handling of the sacrificial elements, both of which are given wholly to God: the blood of the animal being dashed against the sides of the altar, and the body of the animal being consumed by the fire on top of the altar. In this way, the blood provides ransom for the life of the sinner, and the smoke from the offering rises to entreat the face of the deity, whereby it is described as "an aroma pleasing to YHWH." Nevertheless, while this offering was perfectly equipped to deal with man's sin, it was not perfectly equipped to deal with the impact of man's sin upon the deity's property and sanctuary. For this reason, two more offerings were introduced after the giving of the Torah and the Tabernacle at Mt. Sinai.

Unlike the *Olah*, the *Hattat* and the *Asham* were newer offerings, were mandatory, and only appeared after the institution of the sanctuary. A careful reading of the scripture will reveal that these two sacrifices were specifically designed to address two different problems occasioned by sin: desecration, in which the deity's property is profaned, damaged, or destroyed; and defilement, in which the deity's sanctuary is brought into contact with impurity. The *Asham* is best translated "Reparation Offering" (as opposed to "Guilt Offering"), and its primary function was to atone for the desecration of the deity's property. Accordingly, the blood of the animal was dashed against the sides of the altar to provide ransom for the one guilty of desecration, and the flesh of the animal was given as a gift to the sanctuary along with a penalty of one-fifth the cost of whatever had been profaned, damaged, or destroyed. The *Hattat* is best translated "Purification Offering" (as opposed to "Sin Offering"), and its primary function was to atone for the defilement of the deity's sanctuary. Accordingly, the blood of the animal was applied to the parts of the sanctuary that had been defiled, and the flesh of the animal was disposed of outside the camp.

For each of these three sacrifices of atonement, the biblical text provides a full description of the details of their execution, many of which vary depending upon the type of sacrificial animal being used, the financial means of the worshipper, and the gravity of the offense. Thus, sacrifices involving birds, lambs, and oxen all presented unique problems when it came to the matter of how their blood and flesh were to be handled. Moreover, the type of animal to be offered was usually determined with respect to the financial means of the worshipper, the very poor apparently being permitted to substitute a grain offering. And while all offenses rendered the life of the worshipper forfeit, the gravity of the offence could nevertheless be measured with respect to the intentionality with which it was done, the material damages that it caused, and the status of the person who did it. In turn, this was reflected in the severity of the financial penalty placed on the wrongdoer (in cases of desecration), and in the depth to which its impurity penetrated into the sanctuary (in cases of defilement). Over all these details, however, the primary concern of this sacrificial system of atonement was threefold: to preserve the life of man, to maintain the holiness of the deity's property, and to maintain the holiness of the deity's sanctuary.

The Day of Atonement

As mentioned, sacrificial worship is conducted not only on the irregular occasion of man's need or desire, but also on regular occasions established in accordance with the deity's will. Among these set times, the most solemn day in the religious calendar was the annual day of atonement, referred to as Yom Kippur.

The phrase "Yom Kippur" means "Day of Atonement," and was set at the conclusion of the agricultural cycle of the year, specifically on the 10th day of the 7th month. As we shall see, it was a day largely devoted to the activities of the high priest, who served as a representative of the whole community, and on this occasion acted as their intercessor in the sanctuary.

At the beginning of this ritual, the high priest washed his entire body with water, clothed himself in the humble garb of the lay-priest, and selected five animals: four for sacrifice, and one for a "scapegoat." He then engaged in a series of carefully prescribed acts, the fundamental purpose of which was to purge impurity from the sanctuary, the agent of blood being applied to all three of its divisions, and most significantly the adytum where the deity dwelt. Because the gravity of man's transgression was reflected in the degree to which its impurity penetrated into the sanctuary, it was on this occasion alone that those transgressions whose impurity defiled the innermost shrine were atoned for. Thus, this ritual played a central role in the task of keeping the sanctuary a fit dwelling for the deity's presence. Having made purification, the scapegoat was brought forth, the high priest placing his hands on its head, and confessing the sins of himself and the whole community: *Aaron shall lay both his hands upon the head of the live goat and confess over it all the iniquities and transgressions of the Israelites, whatever their sins, putting them on the head of the goat* (Lev. 16:21). Having transferred the impurity of himself and the community onto the head of the goat, he released it in the wilderness: *[The goat] shall be sent off into the wilderness through a designated man. Thus, the goat shall carry on it all their iniquities to an inaccessible region, and the goat shall be set free in the wilderness* (Lev. 16:22).

Although Yom Kippur was for the high priest a day of work, it was for the laity a day of rest. Nevertheless, unlike the various other established days of rest, this one is described as a "sabbath of solemn rest." The uniqueness of this particular sabbath rest consisted in the instruction to "afflict oneself," a phrase traditionally interpreted to mean that the people were to cultivate an attitude of repentance by denying themselves food and by abstaining from sexual relations. In other words, the ritual of atonement conducted in the sanctuary was not intended to stand by itself, but to be accompanied by heartfelt contrition and disciplined self-denial on the part of the people. Atonement is impossible without contrition, and while this particular case involved a mandatory sacrifice, the scripture makes it clear that the contrite individual is the equivalent of one who brings a voluntary sacrifice: *You do not delight in sacrifice, or I would bring it; you do not take pleasure in burnt offerings. The sacrifices of God are a broken spirit; a broken and contrite heart, O God, you will not despise* (Ps. 51:16-17). Furthermore, all genuine seeking of the deity is accompanied by self-denial, since one cannot at the same time reach for the deity and grasp at the world: *For day after day they seek me out; they seem eager to know my ways, as if they were a nation that does right and has not forsaken the commands of its God... The people say "Why have we fasted, and you have not seen it? Why have we humbled ourselves, and you have not noticed?" Yet on the day of your fasting, you do as you please and exploit all your workers* (Is. 58:2-3). Above all else, the purpose of this ritual was to ensure that the deity would continue to rest within his sanctuary: *This is to be a lasting ordinance for you... For on this day, atonement shall be made on your behalf to cleanse you of all your sins: you shall be clean before YHWH. It shall be a sabbath of solemn rest for you, and you shall afflict yourselves; it is a law for all time* (Lev. 16:29-31).

Jesus' Ministry of Sacrificial Atonement

As mentioned in the previous chapter, Jesus' sacrifice not only provides man with water for ablution, but also blood for atonement. *One of the soldiers pierced Jesus' side with a spear, bringing a sudden flow of blood and water. The man who saw it has given testimony, and his testimony is true* (John 19:34-35).

Although Jesus' sacrifice of atonement is perhaps the most familiar aspect of his ministry, the recognition of this has not always been informed by a clear grasp of its mode of operation. In much traditional teaching, atonement is understood solely in terms of providing ransom for the life of the sinner. But as we have seen, atonement is equally about the reparation of the deity's property and the purification of the deity's sanctuary. By extension, Jesus' blood not only ransoms the life of the sinner, but also buys it back and purifies it.

Only in this way can the sacrificial work of atonement be viewed in its proper light, not as an end, but as a beginning. Jesus provides the gift of atonement through his blood in order to prepare man to receive the gift of the divine presence through his body. In this way, he shares the divine life with his disciples, whereby they become sons of God the Father, brothers with God the Son, and vessels of God the Spirit—or, as we have said all along, sanctuaries in which the deity's glory is housed, and icons in which the deity's glory is reflected.

Jesus' Forgiveness of Sinners

Jesus' ministry of atonement is revealed above all in his claim to have authority to forgive sins. In the synoptic tradition, this claim is aptly placed after the story of his ritual purification of the leper: *Some men came, bringing to him a paralytic, carried by four of them. Since they could not get him to Jesus because of the crowd, they made an opening in the roof above Jesus and, after digging through it, lowered the mat the paralyzed man was lying on. When Jesus saw their faith, he said to the paralytic, "Son, your sins are forgiven"* (Mark 2:3-5).

Jesus' claim to forgive sins was immediately recognized as scandalous, since he was attributing to himself a level of authority that had been delegated to the temple by God. Moreover, since forgiveness could only be brought about through sacrificial atonement, his claim also appeared to lack the requisite power. Nevertheless, at a certain point in his ministry, he began to speak to his disciples about the hour of his death, not as an event that was going to happen to him, but as a task that he was going to carry out. In the performance of this task, he made of himself a sacrifice of atonement, whereby he was invested with the power to forgive: *God presented him as a sacrifice of atonement, through faith in his blood* (Rom. 3:25); *He is the atoning sacrifice for our sins, and not only for ours but also for the sins of the whole world* (I John 2:2); *He became a merciful and faithful high priest in service to God, and he made atonement for the sins of the people* (Heb. 2:17).

But what was the nature of this sacrifice of atonement? In the New Testament, it is described simply as "a single sacrifice for sin." By implication, the whole sacrificial system of atonement is concentrated in this single act, whereby it differs from every previous act in that it occurs only once and does the work of them all: *He does not need to offer sacrifices day after day, but he sacrificed for their sins once for all when he offered up himself* (Heb. 7:27). More importantly, however, it fundamentally transforms these sacrifices by directing their work of atonement not to the external effects of sin, but to the internal effects of sin: *For if the blood of goats and bulls and the ashes of a heifer sprinkled on those who are ritually impure sanctify them so that they are outwardly pure, how much more shall the blood of Christ, who through the eternal Spirit, offered himself unblemished to God, purify our consciences from acts that lead to death, so that we may serve the living God* (Heb. 9:13-14).

Thus, Jesus' sacrifice of atonement may be regarded as a unification, interiorization, and perfection of the three sacrifices we have already mentioned. As an *Olah*, it provides ransom for the life of man; as an *Asham*, it provides for the reparation of his soul in order that it might be reclaimed as the deity's property; and as a *Hattat*, it provides for the purification for his soul in order that it might serve as a sanctuary for the deity's presence. In other words, it transforms the functions of the *Olah*, the *Asham*, and the *Hattat* by directing their work toward the interior effects of man's sin, and therefore to the task of rendering him a fit vessel for the housing and glorification the Spirit of God: *It was necessary, then, for the copies of the heavenly things to be purified with these sacrifices, but the heavenly things themselves with better sacrifices than these* (Heb. 9:23); *These sacrifices can never make perfect those who draw near to worship. If they could, would they not have been stopped being offered? For the worshippers would have been cleansed once for all, and would no longer have felt guilty for their sins* (Heb. 10:1-2); *But by one sacrifice he has made perfect forever those who are being made holy* (Heb. 10:14).

Jesus' Priesthood, the Heavenly Sanctuary, and the Deity's Rest

Jesus' sacrificial work not only transforms the *Olah*, the *Hattat*, and the *Asham*, but most profoundly the annual observance of *Yom Kippur*. In the book of Hebrews, he is portrayed not only as a sacrifice of atonement, but also as a great high priest, providing intercession for his people in the heavenly sanctuary, and securing therein a permanent resting place for the presence of the deity: *We do have such a high priest, who serves in the true tabernacle set up by the Lord, and who sat down at the right hand of the throne of the majesty in heaven* (Heb. 8:1-2).

Jesus' authority to serve as a priest owes to his status as the Messiah of Israel. According to the scriptures, the messianic ruler descended from David is declared to be a king as well as a priest "in the order of Melchizedek" (Ps. 110:4). The basis for this declaration is found in David's conquest of Jerusalem, whereby he becomes heir to an ancient dynasty of king-priests who ruled there under the title of "Melchizedek" (Gen. 14:18). According to the book of Genesis, one of the kings of this dynasty received tribute from Abram, and for this reason he came to be regarded as an archetype of the messianic king who would rule over the descendents of Abram: *Christ did not take upon himself the glory of becoming a high priest. But God said to him, "You are my Son, today I have become your Father." And he says in another place, "You are a priest forever, in the order of Melchizedek"* (Heb. 5:5-6).

Yom Kippur presents nothing new in terms of the basic functioning of the sacrifices already mentioned. Rather, its significance lies in the fact that these sacrifices are brought once a year, offered on behalf of the sins of the whole nation, and make atonement for the Most Holy Place. In the same way, Christ's sacrifice was brought in the fullness of time, was offered on behalf of the sins of the whole world, and made atonement in the innermost place of the heavenly sanctuary. Here, the word "heavenly" carries the same sense as the word "spiritual": it is not intended to refer to a place beyond this world, but to the soul of man that exists within this world. As heaven and earth find a point of intersection in the life of the animal, so they find a point of intersection in the soul of man: this is the heavenly sanctuary in which the great high priest made intercession with his own blood to provide atonement—as the text says "purifying our consciences" (Heb. 9:14): *When Christ came as high priest of the good things that are already here, he went through the greater and more perfect tabernacle that is not man-made, that is to say, not part of this creation. He did not enter by means of the blood of goats and calves; but he entered the Most Holy Place once for all by his own blood, having obtained eternal redemption* (Heb. 9:11-12).

As before, the purpose of this rite is to secure the sanctuary as a fit dwelling for the deity's rest. Now, however, it is not in order to secure his dwelling in the temple, but to secure his dwelling in the soul of man. But just as the sacrifice of the old high priest was not intended to stand on its own, but to be accompanied by contrition and self-denial on the part of the people, so the sacrifice of the new high priest is not intended to stand on its own, but to be combined with the contrition and self-denial that accompany faith. For, although the deity's rest has been established forever in the person of Jesus Christ, man does not become a participant in that rest as a matter of course. As with the old Israel led by Joshua (Heb. "Jesus"), so with the new Israel led by Jesus (Grk. "Joshua")—they may both fail to enter into that rest. Hearing must be combined with faith, and authentic faith is always accompanied by repentance and self-denial. It is therefore by faith that his sacrifice provides atonement for the heart, thereby rendering it a fit place for the divine presence to rest. *Therefore, since the promise of entering his rest still stands, let us be careful that none of you be found to have fallen short of it. For we also have had the gospel preached to us, just as they did; but the message they heard was of no value to them because those who heard it did not combine it with faith. But we who have believed have entered into that rest* (Heb. 4:1-3).

CHAPTER FOUR

The Ministry of Sacrificial Communion

There, in the presence of YHWH your God, you and your families shall eat and shall rejoice in everything you have put your hand to, because YHWH your God has blessed you.

Deuteronomy 12:7

The institution of sacrificial worship is often portrayed as though its only function consisted in the provision of blood for atonement. In actual fact, however, its most important function consisted in the provision of food to be used in the sharing of communal meals. It is in the giving and receiving of food that relationship is maintained between YHWH and Israel.

By providing food, the sacrificial system resumes the work of the sanctuary as it was established at creation. It restores mortal man to a life of dependence upon the gracious provision of God: as the garden provided the river, the tree, and the fruit of life, so the tabernacle provides the gift of flesh, bought through the shedding of blood, and thereby satisfying his life-need through the payment of his life-debt. In this way, God's people are sustained not only by his creation, but also by his covenant, whereby they are educated to receive life as a gift given through creaturely sacrifice.

Although the point is often overlooked, man's participation in the sacrificial food of the covenant is the primary means whereby he is marked as ritually holy. This can be seen in the fact that man's entrance into the covenant is secured by his participation in a covenant meal. In the Passover, for example, YHWH's adoption of Israel is put into effect when she partakes of the lamb, the unleavened bread, and the bitter herbs. Moreover, her subsequent life of service in the midst of the deity's sanctuary continues to be maintained through the annual re-enactment of this event, as well as through other regular observances involving the sharing of food. The Lord is holy, his food is holy, and those who eat of it belong to him as his holy people.

Moses' Ministry of Sacrificial Communion

In sacrificial worship of this kind, the most important element is not to be found in the blood, but in the body. Accordingly, the Torah laid down three physical requirements that had to be met by all animals brought to the sacrificial altar: (1) first, they had to be of the appropriate gender, age, and value for the sacrifice in question; (2) second, they had to be of sound body; (3) and third, they had to be ritually pure.

The requirement that the animal be of sound body followed a specific list of criteria (Lev. 22:22-25). Above all, this requirement sought to ensure that the sacrificial gifts being offered would befit the dignity of the deity, a condition that was not always observed: *"If I am a master, where is the respect due me?" says YHWH Almighty... "When you bring blind animals for sacrifice, is that not wrong? When you sacrifice crippled or diseased animals, is not that wrong? Try offering them to your governor! Would he be pleased with you? Would he accept you?" says YHWH Almighty* (Mal. 1:8).

The requirement that the animal be ritually pure specified what kinds of animals were allowed on the altar. According to the biblical text, sacrificial animals were restricted to three local species of livestock (cattle, sheep, and goats), two local species of poultry (dove and pigeon), and excluded all fish. Although the criteria whereby these five animals were set apart is not explicitly mentioned, a careful examination of the animals themselves can furnish the rationale: (1) all were domestic (thus excluding wild animals, among which fish were probably included); (2) all were bred for flesh (thus excluding beasts of burden, such as camels, horses, and donkeys); (3) and all were non-chthonic, meaning that they did not live in, move along, or feed off of the dust of the earth (thus excluding snakes, lizards, pigs, etc.). These criteria ensured that all sacrificial animals would be of the proper value, suitable for food, and devoid of any association with death (that is, with the dust of the earth). The five sacrificial animals that meet these criteria, first mentioned in YHWH's covenant with Abraham (Gen. 15:9), are referred to as the *Lehem Elohim* or "Food of God" (Lev. 21:6), whereby the altar acquires significance as the *Shulhan YHWH* or "Table of the Lord" (Ezek. 44:16). To be sure, YHWH was not regarded as literally eating the flesh of these animals: *Do I eat the flesh of bulls or drink the blood of goats?* (Ps. 50:13). Nevertheless, the language of the table was retained, largely in view of their importance as a source of food for mankind: *The priest shall burn them on the altar as food, an offering made to YHWH by fire* (Lev. 3:11).

The Three Sacrifices for Communion

Now within these parameters, the scripture gives a single name to sacrifices for communion that a person could bring on any occasion they chose, referring to it as the *Zebah Shelamim*. This Hebrew phrase is translated variously as "Well-being Offering," "Peace Offering," or "Fellowship Offering." Unlike the three sacrifices mentioned in the previous chapter, it is for the purpose of maintaining the relationship between man and the deity through the giving and receiving of food.

As befits the purpose of this sacrifice, it was a voluntary offering, brought on one or another occasion of joy, whereby it was divided into three specific types: the freewill offering, used in spontaneous expressions of happiness; the thanksgiving offering, used to express gratitude for the deity's favor; and the votive offering, used to express satisfaction upon the fulfilling of a personal vow to God. On all three of these occasions, the sacrificial elements were handled in the same way: the blood of the animal being dashed against the sides of the altar and so returning its life to God; and the flesh of the animal being shared between the altar, the priests, and the layperson.

The fact that this sacrifice was performed primarily for the purposes of obtaining food provides insight into the larger body of food laws enjoined upon ancient Israel, referred to collectively as "Kashrut." A brief glance at these laws will reveal that they are specifically aimed at man's consumption of meat, that they limit his diet to a select group of animals, and that they are intended to facilitate his ritual holiness. In this way, they provide for the religious organization of the community, so that as one moves into greater proximity with the deity, one draws one's food more and more exclusively from his table. Accordingly, the diet of the priests is the most exclusive of all, for they receive their food solely from the altar, whereby their ration of meat is limited to the five sacrificial animals (Deut. 18:1). The diet of the laity is broader, for they receive their food not only from the altar, but are also permitted to hunt a small variety of wild animals that share similar characteristics with their domestic counterparts (Lev. 11 and Deut. 14). The Gentile is free to eat whatever animal flesh he chooses, though this apparent privilege is precisely an expression for his alienation from YHWH.

Once it is understood that the sanctuary provides the basis for the diet of the surrounding community, the rationale for all of the remaining food laws comes clearly into focus. Thus, the first condition of kosher purity involves proper slaughter, indicating that the people are required to slaughter game the same as they would any sacrificial animal (Lev. 11:39-40). The second condition of kosher purity requires that the priests limit their diet to those animals permissible at the altar, and that the laity limit their diet to these and to those wild animals that shared the same characteristics (Lev. 11 and Deut. 14). And the third condition of kosher purity requires that one refrain from consuming those elements of the animal that are reserved for the altar: the fat of the animal because it is the element that produces a sweet aroma (Lev. 7:22-25); and the blood of the animal because it is the element that makes atonement (Lev. 7:26-27). As for the most peculiar prohibition of all—Do not cook a young goat in its mother's milk (Ex. 23:19b)—the rabbis interpreted this as a general prohibition against mixing meat with dairy, though it probably belongs with the host of other laws forbidding acts of insensitivity against animal life (cf. Ex. 22:29; Lev. 22:27-28; Deut. 22:6-7). In all of these laws, the fundamental purpose was the same: to bind man's life more closely to the sanctuary, to feed him from the table of the Lord, and thereby to render him a creature holy to YHWH (Ex. 22:31; Lev. 11:44-45; 20:22-26; Deut. 14:4-21).

The Passover and the Agricultural Festivals

Although the *Zebah Shelamim* was voluntary, most sacrificial meals were mandatory, being observed at set times throughout the religious calendar. Among these, Passover was the most important, providing for the annual renewal of the covenant between Israel and YHWH. On this first religious observance of the year, the people were required to re-enact the events of the night preceding Israel's exodus from Egypt, whereby they became active participants in the historic tradition that had been handed down to them.

The Passover was observed in the first month of the agricultural year, marked by the coming of spring, the season of rebirth. In preparation for this ritual, each household was to be ritually cleansed by removing from them all products containing leaven. On the fourteenth day of the month, they were to slaughter a lamb: the blood being applied to the entrance-way of the home, and the flesh being roasted over the fire and eaten with unleavened bread and bitter herbs. In this way, provision was made for the two primary aspects of sacrificial worship: atonement and communion. By virtue of the lamb's blood the people's life was spared, and by virtue of the lamb's flesh their life was sustained.

Notwithstanding Passover's importance, it was but the first in a series of ceremonial meals that were to be observed throughout the course of the year. These communal meals took place during the three agricultural festivals, coinciding with the initial ripening, the first produce, and the final ingathering of the harvest. Respectively, they are known as the Feast of Unleavened Bread, the Feast of Weeks, and the Feast of Ingathering. On each of these festal occasions, the people were required to rest from their normal work, to make a pilgrimage to the sanctuary, and to bring offerings to YHWH: *Three times a year all your men must appear before YHWH your God at the place he will choose... No man should appear before YHWH empty-handed: each of you must bring a gift in proportion to the way YHWH your God has blessed you* (Deut. 16:16-17). These mandatory observances were not occasions of solemn repentance, but occasions of joyful thanks: *Be joyful at your feast--you, your sons and daughters, your menservants and maidservants, and the Levites, the aliens, the fatherless and the widows who live in your towns* (Deut. 16:14).

By virtue of the festivals, the food man received from the ground was linked to the sanctuary, and ultimately to the exodus from Egypt. These occasions served to remind the people that they did not own the land, but lived as tenants of the sanctuary, and as serfs of its lord. Unlike other peoples, their natural life was bound to the historical covenant through which they had been delivered from bondage, adopted by the deity, and marked as heirs of his divine estate. As such, the greatest danger to their national identity was that they would become wholly absorbed in natural life and forget their historic roots: *When you eat and are satisfied, and have built fine houses to live in, and your herds and flocks have multiplied, and your silver and gold have increased, and everything you own has prospered, beware lest heart grow proud and you forget YHWH your God, who brought you out of Egypt, out of the land of bondage* (Deut. 8:12-14). Instead, their participation in natural life was to be understood as a gift received in accordance with the terms of their covenant with YHWH: *YHWH brought us out of Egypt with a mighty hand and an outstretched arm, with awesome power and with miraculous signs and portents. He brought us to this place and gave us this land, a land flowing with milk and honey. Wherefore I now bring the first fruits of the soil which you, O YHWH, have given me* (Deut. 26:8-9).

Jesus' Ministry of Sacrificial Communion

Jesus' sacrificial work provides not only blood for atonement, but also flesh for food. *Jesus said to them, "I tell you the truth, unless you drink the blood of the Son of Man and eat his flesh, you have no life in you... The one who feeds on me will live because of me. This is the bread that came down from heaven. You forefathers at manna and died, but he who feeds on this bread will live forever* (John 6:53-58).

In much traditional teaching, the provision of blood for atonement is greatly emphasized, whereas the provision of flesh for food is passed over without much comment. As we have seen, however, the provision of flesh for food was the most important part of the sacrificial system, whereby it not only paid for man's life-debt, but also satisfied his life-need. As we observed in the previous chapter, Jesus' provision of atonement through his blood is precisely in order that he might prepare man to receive the gift of the divine presence through his body.

Although Moses' ministry provided the gift of physical food, Jesus' ministry provides the gift of spiritual food. His body is a source of spiritual food in virtue of the fact that it was selected to be the final resting place of the divine presence. To eat of his flesh is by faith to partake of his sacrifice, and therefore of the impartation of his spirit. And while this transaction takes place in the heart of the individual, it also achieves public expression in the tangible ritual of communion, whereby the community of faith asserts its unity in the breaking of bread. The communion altar is the Table of the Lord, and the bread and wine are the Food of God, and the one who gave his life is the sacrificial lamb "without blemish or defect."

Jesus' Feeding of Sinners

Jesus' ministry of sacrificial communion achieves its initial expression in his custom of "eating with sinners" (Mark 2:13-17). Nevertheless, it is only in his miraculous feeding of the five thousand that he reveals his further intention to feed them from his own hand (Mark 6:30-44). Along with his claim to forgive sin belongs his claim to be the primary breadwinner for the people of God: *Do not work for food that spoils, but for food that endures to eternal life, which the Son of Man will give you* (John 6:27).

In making this claim, Jesus once more ascribes to himself a level of authority that had been delegated to the temple (for the people's food came from the deity, his sanctuary, and its surrounding lands). Moreover, it is once more a claim for which he appears to lack the requisite power (for how could one man provide food for a nation, let alone the whole world?). Jesus' claim naturally raises the question, "What miraculous sign will you give that we may see it and believe you?" And as before, his answer points forward to his sacrificial work on the cross: *I am the bread of life. Your forefathers ate the manna in the desert, yet they died. But here is the bread that comes down from heaven, which a man may eat and not die... This bread is my flesh, which I will give for the life of the world* (John 6:48-51).

But what was the nature of this new sacrificial food? As he himself indicates, it was different from the physical food which their forefathers ate. This was a spiritual food, capable of feeding all men in all places at all times, the likes of which a man could eat "and not die." As such, its fundamental aim did not consist in the nourishment of the body, but in the nourishment of the soul. "To eat of his flesh," therefore, meant by faith to receive the impartation of his spirit, made available through his death on the cross, and declared through his resurrection from the dead to be the Spirit of YHWH. Although the disciples ritually partook of this food at the Last Supper, their real participation in it would not commence until their reception of the promised gift of the Holy Spirit. As Paul observes: *The Kingdom of God is not a matter of eating and drinking, but of righteousness, peace, and joy in the Holy Spirit* (Rom. 14:17).

Thus, Jesus' sacrifice may be regarded as a unification, interiorization, and perfection, not only of the three offerings mentioned in the previous chapter, but also of the *Zebah Shelamim*. As a sacrificial offering for communion, it provides for man's life-need through the gift of food, the eating of which maintains his relationship with the deity, binds his life to the sanctuary, and renders him ritually holy. Now, however, since the gift of flesh has been transformed into a vehicle for the gift of the Spirit, the only food law that remains is the one of exclusive dependence upon the Spirit of Christ. Man's life is no longer sustained by the flesh he receives from the temple, but by the spirit he receives from Christ: *It is good for our hearts to be strengthened by grace, not by ceremonial foods, which are of no value to those who eat them. We have an altar from which those who minister at the tabernacle have no right to eat* (Heb. 13:9-10).

Jesus, the Lamb of God and the Lord of the Harvest

Jesus' sacrificial work took place around the time of the Passover. The night before his death, he spoke at length with his disciples and shared with them the ceremonial meal we have come to refer to as the Last Supper. The purpose of this meal was to clarify the meaning of his impending death by bringing it into direct association with the ritual slaughter of the Paschal Lamb.

As with the Passover ritual, so with this new sacrificial meal. Jesus' flesh was there to provide food: *While they were eating, Jesus took bread, gave thanks and broke it, and gave it to his disciples saying, "Take and eat; this is my body"* (Matt. 26:26). And Jesus' blood was there to provide atonement: *Then he took the cup, gave thanks and offered it to them, saying "Drink from it, all of you. This is my blood of the covenant, which is poured out for many for the forgiveness of sins"* (Matt. 26:27-28). In referring to the institution of a new covenant, he draws attention to the superior nature of his sacrificial work: it provides a more perfect atonement; it provides a more perfect food; and it provides a more perfect communion with God.

And just as Passover inaugurated the agricultural season, so this new sacrifice inaugurates the harvest of human souls for the Kingdom of God. Thus, the disciples' sharing in this sacrificial meal may be identified with the initial ripening of the harvest at the Festival of Unleavened Bread (I Cor. 5:7). The disciples' subsequent receiving of their master's spirit may be identified with the first produce of the harvest at the Festival of Pentecost (Acts 2:1-4). And the production of the full number of disciples upon the earth may be identified with the final ingathering of the harvest at the Festival of Ingathering: *I looked, and there before me was a white cloud, and seated on the cloud was one "like a son of man" with a crown of gold of gold on his head and a sharp sickle in his hand. Then another angel came out of the temple and called in a loud voice to him who was sitting on the cloud, "Take your sickle and reap because the time to reap has come, for the harvest of the earth is ripe." So he who was seated on the cloud swung his sickle over the earth, and the earth was harvested* (Rev. 14:14-16).

Thus, Jesus' Passover initiates the feeding of his people, whereby they are marked as members of the new covenant, and therefore as a people holy to YHWH. Through his blood he washes them of their sin, and through his body he feeds them with the food of the presence of the Holy Spirit. In this way, he advances the deity's kingdom, both extensively as well as intensively: extensively because he establishes a sanctuary for the deity's rest in the souls of all who place their faith in him; and intensively because he thereby enables the saints to find rest for their souls in the interior life of communion with God. It is to this interior life of communion that we now turn, for this concerns not the cultivation of ritual holiness, but the cultivation of moral holiness. As man feeds upon the gift of the divine presence, as he deepens his relationship with God, as he imitates the life of Christ, in such measure does his soul enter more fully into the rest that has been prepared for him: *As the deer pants for streams of water, so my soul pants for you, O God. My soul thirsts for the living God. When can I go and meet with God?* (Ps. 42:1-2).

CHAPTER FIVE

The Ministry of Jesus' Example

I have set you an example that you should do as I have done for you. I tell you the truth, no servant is greater than his master, nor is a messenger greater than the one who sent him. Now that you know these things, you will be blessed if you do them..

John 13:15-17

Jesus' sacrificial work bridges the gap between the sin of man and the holiness of God. He provides water for man's ritual impurity, blood for his moral impurity, and through the gift of his flesh renders him a creature holy to YHWH. Nevertheless, in order for this process of redemption to be brought to completion, man must be possessed not only of ritual holiness, but also of moral holiness.

For this reason, Jesus not only serves as man's mediator, but also as his exemplar. Accordingly, man's redemption reaches its highest expression in the imitation of Christ. To imitate him is to acquire a share in the kind of holiness that comes from submissive obedience to the will of God. Only through submissive obedience can his soul be transformed into a well-governed province within the Kingdom of God.

This, in turn, calls for serious meditation upon his person and work, for if we are to imitate him we must first understand who he is and what he has done. Moreover, such meditation must be of a spiritual nature, for it is not simply a matter of accumulating a sufficient amount of information, but of being able to discern what is essential from what is inessential. As such, this task lies beyond the competence of the purely objective disciplines of philosophy, scholarship, and science, and yet it is a task that lies within the scope of every human being who maintains an infinite interest in the welfare of his soul and the glory of God. From the confessional point of view, Jesus' person consists essentially in the fact that he alone enjoys perfect communion with the deity, and his work consists essentially in the fact that he shares this life of communion with those who place their faith in him.

Jesus' Person

Jesus is described in the classical doctrinal formulations of the church as born of a virgin, conceived by the deity, and therefore as possessing within himself a nature both fully human and fully divine. Nevertheless, the functional significance of these facts only becomes apparent in light of the Old Testament, whereby we understand their role to consist in establishing him as the sanctuary and icon of YHWH.

As the sanctuary, Jesus houses the divine presence within himself: *The Word became flesh and tabernacled among us* (John 1:14a). And as the icon, he reflects the glory of the divine presence: *We have seen his glory, the glory of the One and Only, who came from the Father, full of grace and truth* (John 1:14b). Thus, he accomplishes in himself that for which man and the world were originally created: he serves as the vehicle for housing the glory of the deity, and he serves as the vehicle for reflecting the glory of the deity.

As a house for the divine presence, he is by implication the repository of every grace included within the divine nature: *In*

Christ, all the fullness of the deity lives in bodily form (Col. 2:9). And as a reflection of the divine nature, he is by implication invested with every office necessary for the sharing of these graces: *and you have been given fullness in Christ* (Col. 2:10). In speaking of his person, therefore, we are inevitably drawn into a discussion of the various gifts that accompany the presence of the deity, and the various channels through which these gifts are communicated to mankind.

Jesus' Communion with God

If Jesus is the sanctuary, then his person may be understood on analogy to the interior life of the temple. Like the Most Holy Place, his body houses the presence of the deity, but like the antechamber, he possesses within himself the altar of incense (whereby continual supplication is made to the deity), the menorah (whereby he is provided with the gift of light), and the table of bread (whereby he is provided with the gift of food).

Jesus' life of prayer, for example, may be regarded as an incarnation of the altar of incense. In noting the regularity with which he withdrew from men to pray to God, the scriptures draw attention to the very center of his earthly activity: it was his inner communion with the deity that furnished the wellspring of his outer words and actions. Unlike the previous sanctuary, however, there was no veil separating him from the deity's presence. Moses beheld the divine glory from behind: *[You shall see my back], but my face must not be seen* (Ex. 33:20). But Jesus beheld the divine glory face to face: *No one has ever seen God, but the only begotten Son, who is at the Father's side, has made him known* (John 1:18).

By virtue of Jesus' prayerful communion with the deity, he also partook of the light of the divine presence, signified by the light of the menorah. Here, the image of light serves as a metaphor for the quality of holiness as it achieves expression in the medium of man's understanding. So while the light of holiness is in itself an incomprehensible mystery, when refracted through the prism of the human soul it manifests itself in the full spectrum of spiritual knowledge, wisdom, and experience. Accordingly, the ministry of the one who is said to have walked in the light was vested with the highest possible authority, for he did not receive it from man, but from direct acquaintance with the Word of God: *The Jews were amazed and asked, "How did this man get such learning without having studied?" Jesus answered, "My teaching is not my own. It comes from him who sent me"* (John 7:15-16).

By virtue of Jesus' prayerful communion with the deity, he also partook of the food of the divine presence, signified by the table of bread. Here we have yet another image that serves as a metaphor for the quality of holiness, whereby it emerges not only as the light that illumines man's understanding, but also as the bread that sustains man's life. In other words, the one who is described as eating the bread of heaven received the full measure of his joy, satisfaction, and nourishment from the Word of God: *The tempter came to him and said, "If you are the Son of God, tell these stones to become bread." Jesus answered, "It is written: 'Man does not live by bread alone, but by every word that proceeds from the mouth of God'"* (Matt. 4:3-4). Moreover, it is clear from this passage that he partook of the bread of heaven not merely through his knowledge of the Word, but above all through his obedience to the Word: *Meanwhile, his disciples urged him, "Rabbi, eat something." But he said to them, "I have food you know nothing about: my food is to do the will of him who sent me and finish his work"* (John 4:32-34).

Jesus' Threefold Office

In ancient Israel, the sanctuary served as a palace, an oracle, and a temple. Accordingly, Jesus' person encompassed each of these functions, as well as their associated offices: he was a king, a prophet, and a priest. In this respect, he is foreshadowed by Moses, who also held all three of these offices, but who subsequently distributed them amongst the tribes of Israel. Nevertheless, Jesus is superior to Moses in that he is the reality to which his predecessor pointed: *Moses was faithful in all God's house. Jesus has been found worthy of greater honor than Moses, just as the builder of a house has greater honor than the house itself* (Heb. 3:3).

By Jesus' kingship we refer to his role as steward over the Kingdom of God. This is because his kingship did not consist in the advancement of his own rule, but in the advancement of the rule of God the Father: *For I have come down from heaven not to do my will, but to do the will of the one who sent me* (John 6:38). He was therefore appointed to be a servant, his office being to live in obedience to the will of God, and in this way to realize within himself the governance of the Torah: *He took on the form of a servant... He humbled himself and became obedient unto death... Therefore God exalted him to the highest place and gave him the name that is above every name, that at the name of Jesus every knee should bow and every tongue confess that Jesus Christ is Lord, to the glory of God the Father* (Phil. 2:5-11).

Nevertheless, Jesus' role as king, steward, and servant not only required that he realize the deity's governance within himself, but also that he realize the deity's governance within the lives of others. As a prophet he served as a spokesperson for the deity's word, which is to say his divine covenant, consisting of his eternal law and his temporal acts. And so, just as he did not come to advance his own rule, neither did he come to speak his own word: *I do nothing on my own, but speak only what I have been taught by the Father* (John 8:28). Accordingly, his speech reiterated the terms of the deity's covenant, even as it declared their imminent fulfillment: *Do not think that I have come to abolish the Torah. I have not come to abolish it but to fulfill it. I tell you the truth, until heaven and earth disappear, not the smallest letter will by any means disappear from the Torah until everything is accomplished.* (Matt. 5:17-18).

As a priest, Jesus served as a representative, intercessor, and administrator of grace to mankind. And thus, he did not speak the divine word in judgment of man, but he spoke the divine word as a prelude to his work of standing in man's place, of interceding on his behalf, and of furnishing him with the grace of atonement and communion: *As for the person who hears my words but does not keep them, I do not judge him. For I did not come to judge the world, but to save it* (John 12:47). It is therefore not only through his prophetic activity, but especially through his priestly activity that the governance of the deity passes from his life into the lives of his disciples: *For what the Torah was powerless to do in that it was weakened by the sinful nature, God did by sending his own Son in the likeness of sinful man to be a sin offering. And so he condemned sin in sinful man in order that the righteous requirements of the Torah might be met in us, who do not live according to the sinful nature, but according to the Spirit* (Rom. 8:3-4).

Jesus' Work

Jesus' person provides the basis for how we should interpret his work. As the true sanctuary he houses the glory of the deity, and as the true icon he is equipped to reflect the glory of the deity through his investiture as king, prophet, and priest.

Jesus' work, therefore, may be said to consist in advancing the deity's kingdom by discharging the duties included within each of these three offices. From a historical point of view, it can be divided into three periods: (1) the ministry of his life, during which he traveled, taught, and performed various miraculous signs; (2) the ministry of his death, in which he suffered, was crucified, and buried; (3) and the ministry of his resurrection, in which he was raised to life, appeared to the disciples, and ascended to the right hand of God the Father.

All three of these periods are of equal importance for the advancement of the Kingdom of God. Jesus' living ministry bears witness to the kingdom as taught by the example of his own life. His sacrificial death does this as well, in addition to its previously mentioned function of providing a sacramental mediator between the sinfulness of man and the holiness of God. As for his resurrection from the dead, this serves not only as a vindication of his claim to be the sanctuary of the deity (i.e., through the power of an indestructible life, Heb. 7:16), but also to establish him as the firstborn of the new heaven and the new earth (i.e., the firstfruits of those who have fallen asleep, I Cor. 15:20).

The Ministry of Jesus' Life

In Jesus' three year ministry, his words and deeds give expression to all three of his divine offices. In the following section, each are dealt with separately, though careful reflection will reveal that they interpenetrate one another at every level, so that they can only be regarded as names for different aspects of a single unitary vocation.

Jesus' kingship is of first importance in the gospels. He realizes the kingdom of heaven on earth by fulfilling the terms of the covenant between man and YHWH. This begins with his baptism, wherein he agrees to take up the sin of mankind, after which he suffers the temptation of mankind for a period of forty days. By virtue of his perfect obedience to the commandments, he ushers in the perfect blessing that was promised: the divine presence in the midst of the fallen world.

Jesus' prophetic ministry follows. Having realized the kingdom of heaven within himself, he begins his public ministry with the proclamation, "The Kingdom of God is near." Jesus expounds on the nature of the Kingdom of God in his parables, the cardinal example of which is the Parable of the Sower: the Gospel is the seed of the kingdom; the prophetic messenger sows the seed of the kingdom; and the recipient is the soil in which the kingdom either flourishes or withers. In Jesus' Sermon on the Mount, he provides the most exhaustive account of the nature of the Kingdom of God: designating his own role as the fulfiller of the commands of the Torah, designating his followers as the recipients of the promised blessings of the Torah, and expounding on the life of discipleship as a life of prayer, virtue, self-denial, mercy, charity, and joy.

As for Jesus' priestly ministry, this consists not in the administration of words but of grace. This administration of grace consists first and foremost in acts of physical and mental healing, which serve not only to benefit the one healed, but to point to the identity of their healer: *[YHWH] upholds the cause of the oppressed and gives food to the hungry. YHWH sets the prisoners free, YHWH gives sight to the blind, YHWH lifts up those who are bowed down, YHWH loves the righteous. YHWH watches over the alien and sustains the fatherless and the widow, but he frustrates the ways of the wicked* (Ps. 146:7-9). Perhaps most important of all, these acts of physical and mental healing serve the religious function of enabling persons to draw near to God: as in the healing of ritual impurity (e.g., death, decay, and irregular sexual discharges), and as in the healing of moral impurity (e.g., the casting out of bad, evil, or impure spirits). Ultimately, however, the purpose of bringing them near is so that they might be brought into union with God: (1) first, through the forgiveness of sins (an anticipation of the gift of his sacrificed life [Mk 2:5]); (2) and second, through the sharing of food (an anticipation of the gift of his resurrected life [Mk 2:15]). In this way, Jesus' three year ministry points forward to the events of Passion Week, even as it points back to the defining events in the history of Israel: it marks the beginning of a new exodus, a new mountain, and a new law and sanctuary.

The Ministry of Jesus' Death

Near the end of his three year ministry, Jesus began to tell his disciples about the events that were about to take place on what we now refer to as Passion Week: *He then began to teach them that the Son of Man must suffer many things and be rejected by the elders, chief priests, and teachers of the Torah, and that he must be killed and after three days rise again* (Mk 8:31).

At the beginning of Jesus' ministry, his kingship achieved its first expression in his obedient resistance to temptation. Now, at the end of his ministry, it achieves expression in his obedient perseverance under trial: his willingness to suffer the agony of the cross in fulfillment of his earthly mission. Accordingly, this does not take place in the desert of Judea (a place of scarcity), but in the garden of Gethsemane (a place of abundance), and once more he fulfills the requirements of the covenant by subordinating his natural desire—"Father, save me from this hour"—to his spiritual desire—"Father, glorify your name." Again, his obedience at this point is not only in order that the deity's governance might be manifest in him, but in order that the deity's governance might be manifest in the lives of his disciples: *I tell you the truth, unless a kernel of wheat falls to the ground and dies, it remains only a single seed. But if it dies, it produces many seeds* (John 12:24).

After Jesus' time of testing in the garden, he is arrested, tried, and sentenced to death. Here, in the clash between his self-testimony and man's counter-testimony, we find the culmination of his prophetic ministry. As before, he proclaims the coming of the kingdom, indicating that its power does not lie in external force, but in the internal witness it gives to the truth: *Jesus said, "My kingdom is not of this world. If it were, my servants would fight to prevent my arrest by the Jews... I came into the world, to testify to the truth: everyone on the side of truth listens to me"* (John 18:36-37). Now, however, he publicly testifies that he is the king of the Jews, the Messiah, the Son of God, and therefore the one through whom the deity will reassert his rule over all of mankind: *The high priest asked him, "Are you the Christ, Son of the Blessed One?" "I am," said Jesus. "And you will see the Son of Man sitting at the right hand of the Mighty One and coming on the clouds of heaven"* (Mark 14:61-62). And herein lies the full revelation of the Word of God: *For the testimony of Jesus is the spirit of prophecy* (Rev. 19:10).

At last, we come to the events of Jesus' Passion. Here we find the culmination of all that we have hitherto referred to as his priestly ministry: he prays on man's behalf, he sacrifices himself on man's behalf, and in this way becomes an administrator of divine grace. His first words from the cross point to the forgiveness he is empowered to bestow by virtue of his blood: *Jesus said "Father, forgive them, for they do not know what they are doing"* (Luke 23:34). And his words to the thief who was crucified with him points to the divine fellowship he is empowered to bestow by virtue of the spirit residing within his body: *Jesus said "I tell you the truth, today you will be with me in paradise"* (Luke 23:43). In this mysterious statement, we find an anticipation of the resurrection, for the gift of his spirit not only provides fellowship with the deity in the present life, but ensures fellowship with the deity in the life to come: *And if the same spirit that raised Jesus from the dead dwell in you, then he who raised him from the dead will also give life to your mortal bodies through the spirit that lives in you* (Rom. 8:11).

In all of the foregoing, we may observe an organic unity in the life of Jesus Christ. By virtue of his communion with the deity, he participates in the divine light, and by walking in accordance with that light he partakes of the bread of heaven: first, by realizing the governance of the deity within himself; and second, by realizing the governance of the deity within others. In short, there is in the manifold variety of elements we have discussed a divine simplicity for which there exists no name, except it be the name of Jesus Christ. He is therefore a mystery, and yet the scriptures provide in the sanctuary a language whereby we may speak of his person and work, not in order that we may comprehend him, but in order that we may imitate him: we are to become sanctuaries for the divine presence, to partake of the graces of fellowship, light, and food, to serve as kings, prophets, and priests, and to share in the fellowship of his sufferings, the hope of his resurrection, and the blessedness of his rest.

PART III
THE DESTINY OF MAN
MADE ACTUAL

CHAPTER ONE

The Doorway of Faith

*Without faith it is impossible to please God, because
anyone who comes to him must believe that he exists, and
also that he rewards those who earnestly seek him.*

Hebrews 11:6

In part one, we said the deity exercises his rule over creation through his sanctuary and icon, and that these are ultimately to be found in the soul of man. In other words, the human race exists in order that it might house and reflect the glory of God.

In part two, we asked how it was possible for a holy deity to take up his residence within sinful man without causing defilement to his holiness and destruction to the sinner. The answer was found to consist in the fourfold ministry of Jesus Christ, which provides water for man's ritual impurity, blood for his moral impurity, flesh for his ritual holiness, and an example that he should follow in leading a life of moral holiness.

In part three, we now address the question of how this is to be made actual in the life of man. Here at last we arrive at the concept of faith, that mysterious act whereby the work of redemption is applied to the life of the individual person. It is by faith that we are transformed into sanctuaries and redeemed as icons, wherein consists the salvation of man and the glorification of God. It is called salvation because it delivers man from sin, and it is called glorification because it delivers man over to God. To be delivered over to God means to belong to him as ritually holy and to glorify him by leading lives that are morally holy, which again consists in the imitation of Jesus Christ, who is the only begotten Son of the Father.

On Repentant Faith

In Jesus' ministry, he taught that the doorway to the heavenly kingdom is unlocked with the keys of repentance and belief: *The time is fulfilled; the Kingdom of God has come near; repent and believe the good news* (Mk 1:15).

As to the nature of this kingdom, the popular view that its restoration would consist in liberation from evil rulers was not far from the truth, for the lord of all evil rulers was indeed the power of sin itself. This was the tyrant who ruled over all men, the one from whom man was most in need of liberation, and the one whose power was broken in the gospel of Jesus Christ: *Jesus said, "If I drive out demons by the finger of God, then the Kingdom of God has come upon you"* (Lk 11:20).

As to the call to repent and believe, this had already enjoyed a long career in the history of the God's covenant with Israel. The call to repent was an invitation to return to his covenant, and the call to believe was a reminder that such return could only begin with an acknowledgment of the word upon which his covenant was based. God rules over man through his word, and this word implicitly commands belief, whereby it is granted access to the mind. In other words, belief is the most primitive form of obedience, and indeed the one upon which all subsequent forms of obedience depend. Abraham provides the supreme example of this: in believing the promise that he would be made into a great nation, he became obedient to the implicit command to believe, and this in turn furnished the rationale for his obedience to the explicit command to leave his native home and go to a foreign country.

The Nature of Repentance

As mentioned, the act of repentance can be understood as one of turning back to the covenant (Heb. *shuv*): *If you seek YHWH your God, you will find him, if only you seek for him with all your heart and all your soul. When you are in distress because all these things have happened to you, then in later days you will return to YHWH your God and obey him* (Deut. 4:29-30).

For Gentiles, such return took the form of religious conversion. As individuals who were alienated from the deity's word, they could only return to his word by making the decision to enter into his covenant. Indeed, long before the time of Jesus or John the Baptist, this decision to convert had already come to be signified by the ritual of baptism, whereby the individual made a symbolic journey through the waters of the Red Sea with Moses and Israel.

For the Israelites, however, return took the form of recommitment to the covenant and restoration through the system of sacrificial atonement provided by the temple. Nevertheless, only the nation's continued faithfulness to the covenant could ensure the continued efficacy of the temple. If the nation's sins should extend so far as to corrupt the temple, it would cease to serve as a sanctuary for the deity's presence, and therefore as a repository for his divine grace. And this is in fact what happened to Israel: YHWH removed himself from the sanctuary, thereby enabling its eventual destruction. In the wake of these events, repentance assumed the more austere form of national confession and hopeful expectation of a messiah who would bring with him a more perfect temple, a more perfect covenant, and a more perfect kingdom.

Thus, when John the Baptist came, immersing both Gentiles and Jews, it was a clear indication that he was calling people away not only from paganism, but also from their broken covenant and failed system of temple worship. Contrary to the suspicions of the religious leaders of the time, this did not amount to an abolition of the covenant, but rather pointed to its imminent fulfillment in the satisfaction of all its commands and promises. This was to be found in the person of Jesus Christ, who would lead his people out of the bondage of sin and into the kingdom of holiness through the sanctuary of his own self. And thus, the call to repentance was a call to turn away from every form of life found outside the protection of the Messiah of Israel—in him alone was the final resting place of YHWH.

The Nature of Faith

As for faith, this is not to be confused with man's belief in the existence of a higher power, for that can assume a variety of different forms. Although such belief is important, it is really only a precondition of faith, and rather constitutes an object of experiential and rational knowledge: *For since the creation of the world, God's invisible qualities—his eternal power and divine nature—have been clearly seen, being understood from what has been made, so that men are without excuse* (Rom. 1:20).

In the Old Testament, biblical faith was specifically directed to the god who revealed himself in the historical covenant with Israel. Therefore, to have faith meant to believe in the word of his covenant, and to entrust oneself to the word of his covenant. This act of faith presupposed a certain amount of god-knowledge as well as a certain amount of self-knowledge, for no one enters into a trust without first becoming acquainted with their prospective trustee, and no one entrusts to another what they feel perfectly well equipped to handle on their own. Thus, the preconditions of faith may be said to consist in the knowledge of God's holiness and the knowledge of one's own sinfulness, which are the basis of godly fear and humility, and therefore of the spirit of repentance. This is the narrow road that leads to faith: not an inference drawn on the basis of outward facts, but a resolution that ripens as the fruit of one's interior history.

In the New Testament, biblical faith refers more specifically to the person of Jesus Christ, and in three distinct senses. First, it means to believe his claim that the kingdom has come, and therefore that he is the true sanctuary and icon of God (*assensus*). Second, it means to trust in him for all the graces of the sanctuary, meaning thereby the grace of forgiveness and the grace of the divine presence (*fiducia*). And third, it means to remain within the grace of the divine presence by continually fixing the eye of the mind upon God (*intueor*). Faith therefore has a theoretical, a practical, and an aesthetic dimension, whereby by it exercises an influence on the way man thinks, the way he acts, and even the way he experiences life. Like Abraham, the man of faith believes God, he trusts God, and he leaves behind his godless way of life for a godly way of life, a life lived in the imitation of Christ.

Ultimately, then, faith brings man into a condition of interior fellowship with God. It is the doorway through which the deity gains access to man's soul, and it is the doorway through which man enters into that sanctuary to engage in a life of unceasing worship before the deity's holy presence. It is therefore not a transient act, but a continuing act, wherein the scriptures declare that "The righteous will live by faith."

The Life of Union with God

By faith man becomes a participant in the grace of forgiveness and the grace of the divine presence, whereby he is redeemed as a "son of God" (John 1:12). Nevertheless, this does not simply amount to a restoration of his condition prior to the fall, for in addition to being redeemed as the deity's icon, he has also been transformed into the deity's sanctuary. As a result, he now enters into a level of intimacy with the deity beyond that of his ancestors, who bore only an external relation to the sanctuary.

Here again we see that man's salvation does not consist only in his being delivered from sin, but also in his being brought into organic union with the life of the Triune God. He is like a branch that has been grafted onto a vine: the deity imparts to him its life, and he in turn becomes a participant in the life of the deity. This union of man with the deity, referred to as *theosis* in Greek, and as *divinization* in Latin, finds its oldest precedent in the *shekhinah* of the Hebrews. It is the divine presence that first took up its abode in the Tabernacle, then in the person of Christ, and finally comes to rest in the soul of the believer. As the scripture declares: *He has given us his very great and precious promises, so that through them you may participate in the divine nature* (II Pet. 1:4).

As a result of man's union with the deity, he is now initiated into a living relationship with the Triune God. His life is justified before the Father, and progressively sanctified unto the likeness of the Son, all through the power of the indwelling Spirit. To say that his life is justified is to say that it has been accepted as ritually holy, and to say that it is progressively sanctified is to say that it is in the process of becoming morally holy—again, by virtue of the power of the indwelling Holy Spirit. The gift of atonement is in order to prepare the way for the indwelling Spirit, apart from which there is no union with Christ: *If anyone does not have the Spirit of Christ, he does not belong to Christ* (Rom. 8:9). And apart from union with Christ, there is neither justification nor sanctification: *You were washed, you were sanctified, and you were justified in the name of our Lord Jesus Christ and by the Spirit of our God* (I Cor. 6:11).

Justification

Justification is a term that refers to a judges' act of declaring the accused to be in right standing before the law. Although it is a forensic term, it is not on that account foreign to the sanctuary, which served as the palace of the deity, and therefore as the seat of his executive, legislative, and judicial authority. YHWH's governance went forth from his temple: a copy of the law was placed in the sanctuary (Ex. 25:16); the teaching of the law took place at the sanctuary (Lev. 10:11); and the supreme court of justice assembled at the sanctuary (cf. Ex. 18 and Deut. 17:8-13).

Accordingly, YHWH was regarded as the great king, lawmaker, and judge over all the earth. The terms of his rule were to be found in his covenant with mankind, and therefore righteousness came to be understood as the quality of being faithful to its requirements. For the Gentile, this meant living up to the light of his conscience, which retained a remnant of the divine image (Rom. 2:14). For the Jew, this meant living up to the light of the Torah, which demanded trust and obedience to the Word of YHWH (Rom. 2:13). And for YHWH, it meant being faithful to his covenant promise, to restore his rule upon the earth, and therefore to judge sin and to bring all nations back into communion with himself. As we have seen, however, man was unable to satisfy the requirements of the covenant, whereby his faith came to rest its hope upon the righteousness of God: *All have turned aside, they have together become corrupt; there is no one righteous, not even one* (Ps. 14:3). Accordingly, the ancient prophets spoke of a coming "Day of the Lord," a day when the great ruler of the earth would reveal his righteousness by restoring his kingdom upon the earth, by crushing the power of sin, and by reconciling himself to all people: *The Torah will go out from me; my justice will become a light to the nations. My righteousness draws near speedily, my salvation is on the way, and my arm will bring justice to the nations* (Is. 51:4-5).

In the New Testament, Paul argues that YHWH's faithfulness to the terms of his covenant has been revealed in the gospel of Jesus Christ: *But now, apart from the Torah, the righteousness of God has been revealed, to which the Torah and the Prophets bear witness* (Rom. 3:21). In Jesus' perfect obedience, the Father is honored as the sovereign ruler over all creation: *Being found in appearance as a man, he humbled himself and became obedient unto death—even death on a cross* (Phil. 2:8). In Jesus' sacrificial death, the Father executes his judgment upon sinful man: *God presented him as a sacrifice of atonement... He did this to demonstrate his justice, because in his forbearance he had left the sins committed beforehand unpunished* (Rom. 3:25). And in Jesus' resurrection, the Father transforms sinful man into a creature wholly free from the power of sin and wholly fitted for communion with God: *Christ has indeed been raised from the dead, the firstfruits of those who have fallen asleep* (I Cor. 15:20). This then is justification: as the Father accepts the Son, so he accepts all who have been joined to the Son, which is to say all who by faith participate in the grace won by his sacrifice: they have received atonement through the blood that came from his death, and they have been brought into communion with the deity through the spirit that raised him from the dead: *He was delivered over to death for our sins and was raised to life for our justification* (Rom. 4:25).

For Christians, the doctrine of justification is one of the most important parts of their understanding of the gospel: it is the doctrine whereby they are assured that they are free from divine condemnation and members of the covenant people of God. Nevertheless, there has crept into many of its formulations a privileging of the blood of Christ over the Spirit of Christ, whereby the whole transaction of religious conversion has been made to consist in the acceptance of forgiveness without the acceptance of the Spirit. Unfortunately, these are not the terms that the God of the covenant offers: we are forgiven in order that we might be filled with his presence, and we are not given the option of accepting the one and declining the other. Only the one who has accepted both is justified, and the indwelling spirit whereby he is regarded as ritually holy will just as assuredly set him on the path to moral holiness.

Sanctification

If justification means that one is accepted as ritually holy, then sanctification means that one is also in a process of becoming morally holy. By faith the believer has received the divine presence into their heart, and by faith the believer now enters into a life of ever-deepening communion with God. These are not two separate works of grace, but different stages in the unfolding of a single work of grace, different aspects of man's unification with the Triune God.

This union has its origin in the deity's love, whereby he shares his holy presence with mankind. In turn, it is the means through which he creates in the heart of man a love of himself: *We love him because he first loved us* (I John 4:19). Thus, the motive that drives the individual along the road of sanctification is furnished by his initial reception of the Spirit. In tasting of the deity there is awakened in him a profound hunger for an even deeper experience of God: *As the dear pants for streams of water, so my soul longs for thee, O God. My soul thirsts for God, for the living God* (Ps. 42:1-2). This is the paradox of man's loving pursuit of God, that having found him, he nevertheless continues to seek after him.

The outworking of this pursuit consists in the cultivation of all that is godly, and in the crucifixion of all that is godless. The cultivation of godliness consists in what the older devotional literature referred to as the imitation of Christ: *Put on the Lord Jesus Christ, and do not make provision for the flesh, to fulfill the lusts therefore* (Rom. 13:14). The crucifixion of godlessness consists in what the older devotional literature referred to as the mortification of the flesh: *For if you live according to the flesh, you will die; but if by the Spirit you mortify the misdeeds of the body, you will live* (Rom. 8:13). In other words, the individual who has tasted of the heavenly gift nevertheless retains a love of both himself and the world, and therefore he must work to encourage the life of the new man and discourage the life of the old man: *For the flesh desires what is contrary to the Spirit, and the Spirit what is contrary to the flesh—they are in conflict with each other so that you do not do what you want* (Gal. 5:17). It is a journey of continual death and rebirth, a journey that involves self denial and suffering, but one that is nevertheless attended with inexpressible peace and joy.

In Christianity today, one seldom hears about this inner journey of progress in holiness. Just as justification has been made to consist in the acceptance of the blood of Christ without the Spirit of Christ, so sanctification has been made to consist in the doing of various external deeds without the inner deeds through which alone the heart is transformed. According to Jesus' teaching, however, the deity's kingdom does not have its basis in the outer world of space and time, but in the inner world of the human soul: *The Kingdom of God does not come with your careful observation, nor will people say "Here it is," or "There it is," because the Kingdom of God is within you* (Luke 17:20-21). And yet, it does not on this account fail to exercise an influence on the external world, but rather exercises the greatest influence of all: *The Kingdom of God is like a mustard seed, which is the smallest seed you plant in the ground. Yet when planted, it grows and becomes the largest of all garden plants, with such big branches that the birds of the air can perch in its shade* (Mk 4:31-32).

CHAPTER TWO

The Incense of Prayer

Take my prayer as an offering of incense.

Psalm 141:2

Jesus is the sanctuary of God. His death and resurrection are the means whereby he shares the divine presence with his disciples, the greatest of the divine graces to which they gain access through the door of faith.

But just as they have received the divine presence by faith, so they must continue to cultivate its presence by faith. In other words, faith is not a transient act, but a continuing act, and therefore expresses itself in a life of continual communication with God: *Remain in me, and I will remain in you. No branch can bear fruit in itself; it must remain in the vine* (John 15:4).

For the Christian, this life of continuing communication takes the form of prayer. As the altar of incense was kept continually burning, so the altar of prayer is to be kept continually burning: always entreating the face of the deity, and always maintaining communion with God: *Aaron shall burn aromatic incense on the altar: he shall burnt it every morning when he tends the lamps, and he shall burn at twilight when he lights the lamps—a regular incense offering before YHWH throughout the ages* (Ex. 30:7-8).

The Nature of Prayer

Prayer in its most basic form has a beautiful childlike quality about it. It requires nothing more than a pouring out of the heart in conversation with the deity. And yet, for all its simplicity, a profound depth is revealed in the human soul when it reaches beyond itself, indeed beyond the limits of its own world, and stretches out into the infinite mystery of God.

Although man ought never to outgrow his capacity for prayer of this kind, as he matures it will necessarily begin to take on the character of a more regular discipline. Indeed, for the one who truly hungers after godliness, it will prove to be the most fundamental disciple of his spiritual life, engaging the whole of his being, and including every faculty of his mind: theoretical, practical, and aesthetic. In other words, it is the highest activity of which man is capable.

Christian prayer is unique in that it is not only a means of communicating with the deity, but also a means of achieving a deeper consciousness of one's union with the Trinitarian Godhead. The believer who prays to God the Father, through the mediation of the Son, and in the indwelling power of the Holy Spirit, is essentially immersing himself in the life of God. In prayer he is not so much acting as acted upon, all of his thoughts, resolutions, and feelings being brought under the influence of the all-pervading presence of the holy deity.

The Basic Form and Content of Prayer

Prayer is a communication, and therefore its most fundamental elements consist in the acts of speaking and listening. In the act of speaking man discloses himself to God, and in the act of listening he becomes the recipient of the deity's self-disclosure to man. It is a relationship based on mutual self-revelation, the depth of which cannot be plumbed in any single encounter, nor even in a lifetime of repeated encounters, but beckons man onward into an infinite and eternally deepening fellowship with God.

The first element in communication is speaking, the most natural form of which is verbal prayer, and the most basic content of which is man's self-disclosure to God. And yet, the man who speaks does not do so in order to inform God, but rather to confide in God. In the act of confiding, he steps out of the prison of his own I and into the freedom of openness before the eternal Thou. Moreover, it is by virtue of this act that the deity's foreknowledge about him is transformed into a more intimate acquaintanceship with him. The man of prayer is not a man who broods within himself, nor a man who holds back some things while sharing others, but a man who lays everything at the feet of his lord: his fears and hopes, his successes and failures, his thanksgivings and petitions, and most of all his anguish over sin and his longing for holiness.

The second element in communication is listening, the most natural form of which is meditation, and the basic content of which is God's self-disclosure to man. The man who meditates does not speak, but fixes the attention of his mind on the Word of God. For the deity is not silent, but speaks continually from eternity into the midst of the temporal world. He speaks through creation, through his covenant, and through the spirit which he makes to indwell his sanctuary. All of these are the living, breathing, and speaking institutions to which his written word bears witness. Accordingly, it is through these living institutions, and through the testimony of the written word, that man in the strictest sense receives an answer to his prayers. The question is not whether the deity answers, but whether man will take the time to listen to what is being said to him—will he take the time to meditate?

As important as it is to set aside certain places and times for speaking and listening, this relationship of mutual self-revelation is one that cannot be confined to particular places and times, and indeed it lies beyond the competence of language to fully articulate or comprehend. Accordingly, the truly hungry soul will naturally seek to place these disciplines within the context of a more all-encompassing relationship with God. For a great many saints throughout the ages, this more all-encompassing relationship has taken the form of contemplative prayer, the practice of directing one's attention always and everywhere to the abiding presence of God: *I am always mindful of the presence of YHWH. He is at my right hand. I will not be shaken* (Ps. 16:8). By keeping the inward eyes of their heart focused on the deity's presence here and now, the believer enters into that dimension of reality which he has already taken hold of by faith: *And the name of the city from that time on will be "The Lord is There"* (Ezek. 48:35). As on a moment-by-moment basis the believer gazes upon the face of the deity, so he will become aware that the deity's countenance is turned toward him, and will discover in this silent acknowledgment of one another both the simplest as well as the richest form of communication between himself and God. For the fullness of all that the deity could ever says is disclosed in the gift of his abiding presence: *God has sent into our hearts the Spirit of the Son that cries "Father!"* (Gal. 4:6). And the fullness of all that we could ever say is disclosed in the light of the same: *O YHWH, you have searched me and you know me. You know when I sit and when I rise; you perceive my thoughts from afar. You discern my going out and my lying down; you are familiar with all my ways. Before a word is on my tongue, you know it completely, O YHWH* (Ps. 139:1-4).

The Fundamental Purpose of Prayer

Thus, the man who prays enters into conscious filial communication with God the Father. At this point, the skeptic might ask "If we've already been made sons of God, what is the point of cultivating an awareness of the fact?" But here we must call to mind the distinction between ritual and moral holiness, for although it is certainly true that we have been made sons in a ritual sense, we have not yet been made sons in a moral sense. This, then, is the fundamental purpose of prayer: it is the means of our moral sanctification, of the conditioning of our thoughts, feelings, and resolutions, and of bringing our will into conformity with the will of God.

Prayer's first item of business is the education of the head. If my will is to be conformed to the will of God, I must know what his will is: *My people are destroyed for lack of knowledge* (Hos. 4:6). More than that, I must be reminded of what his will is, for the heart of idolatry consists not only in ignorance, but in man's chronic forgetfulness and failure to remember: *Only be careful, and watch yourselves closely to that you do not forget the things your eyes have seen or let them slip from your heart as long as you live... Remember the day you stood before YHWH your God at Horeb* (Deut. 4:9-10). At this point, man's speaking gives way to listening, not because there is any question about the deity's love for him, but because there is a very real question about his love for the deity: will he be found willing to submit himself to the will of God? If the will of man is to be brought into conformity with the will of God, then this can only take the form of humble submission, as expressed in the prayer " Not my will, but thy will be done." And yet, the purpose is not to over-ride man's petitions, but to transform them so that they are identical with the will of God.

Accordingly, prayer's second item of business is the education of the heart. If my will is to be conformed to the will of God, I must not only know what his will is, but I must also desire to do his will: *And I will give you a new heart and put a new spirit into you: I will remove the heart of stone from your body and give you a heart of flesh, and I will put a new spirit into you. Thus, I will cause you to follow my decrees and faithfully to observe my laws* (Ezek. 36:26-27). Having tasted of the heavenly gift, and having hungered after the divine presence, man must continue to feed upon it if he is to grow his appetite for holiness: *Taste and see how good is YHWH; happy is the man who takes refuge in him* (Ps. 34:8).

For just as the godlessness of the mind gives power to sin, so the cultivation of a godly mind gives power to holiness. Man may be possessed of a deep sense of obligation, but unless his desires have been thoroughly conditioned by his conscience, he will always lack the power to carry out the commands issued by his better part. To do what is right with grit teeth is not devoid of value, but it will only prove successful for lesser trials and temptations, whereas the one possessed of true spiritual power is the one who has learned to take a hearty joy in holy living.

Prayer's third item of business is the education of the hands. If my will is to be conformed to the will of God, I must not only desire to do his will, but I must also resolve to act upon it. Thus, in the final analysis, prayer is an inward activity that manifests itself in outward deeds, and specifically in the administration of man's threefold office as prophet, priest, and king.

The Lord's Prayer

For Christians, the *Pater Noster*, "Our Father," or "Lord's Prayer," provides the ideal pattern of prayer. Although it is a spoken prayer, it is speech that has been born of listening, giving profound expression to the self-disclosure of both man as well as God. Moreover, the simplicity of its language provides material that is suited not only for immediate comprehension, but also for the more reflective disciplines of meditation and contemplation.

In the Gospels, the Lord's Prayer is provided in response to the request of the disciples, "Lord, teach us to pray": *One of his disciples said to him, "Lord, teach us to pray, just as John taught his disciples." He said to them, "When you pray, say: Father, hallowed by your name, your kingdom come. Give us each day our daily bread. Forgive us our sins, for we also forgive everyone who sins against us. And lead us not into temptation"* (Lk 11:2-4).

From antiquity to the present, all of the greatest theologians have turned to this model as providing the best source of guidance for the spiritual life of man: *Do not pray like the hypocrites, but rather as the Lord commanded in his Gospel* (Didache); *Whatever else we say when we pray, if we pray as we should, we are only saying what is already contained in the Lord's Prayer* (Augustine); *The Pater Noster was taught us by Christ himself; it was also the only prayer he taught us to say; and he gave it to us in answer to the request of his disciples, "Lord, teach us to pray"* (Aquinas); *To this day, I nurse at the Lord's Prayer like a child, as an old man eat and drink from it and never get my fill: it is the very best prayer, even better than the Psalter, which is so very dear to me* (Luther); *God prescribed a form for us in which is set forth as in a table all that he allows us to seek of him, all that is of benefit to us, all that we need to ask: it is the prayer which the heavenly Father has taught us through his beloved Son* (Calvin); *Jesus calls us, allows us, commands us to speak with him to God, to pray his prayer with him, to be united with him in the Lord's Prayer* (Barth).

The Initial Address

The Lord's Prayer immediately invites the disciple into the mind of Christ: *"For who has known the mind of the Lord that he may instruct him." But we have the mind of Christ* (I Cor. 2:16).

Now the mind of Christ is the doing of the will of the Father: *"My food," said Jesus, "is to do the will of him who sent me and to finish his work"* (John 4:34). This, in turn, consists in the Kingdom of God, established through his covenant, and manifested in obedience to his commands and in the promised blessing of fellowship with him, all of which finds satisfaction in Jesus Christ. Accordingly, Jesus' prayer begins by addressing itself to the god of the covenant, revealed as creation's otherworldly ruler in the first two of the Ten Commandments.

Moreover, this initial "Our Father" indicates that man's speaking is born out of the redemptive work of Jesus Christ. For the Bible does not assume as a matter of course that man is a son of God, but rather that man is an enemy of God. In other words, this address can only really be spoken by Christ, or by the one who has been made a brother with Christ: *For those God foreknew he also predestined to be conformed to the likeness of his Son, that he might be the firstborn among many brothers* (Rom. 8:29). The Lord's Prayer is distinctively Christian: it cannot be prayed by just anyone, but only by those who are in communion with the Father through the intercession of the Son and the indwelling gift of the Holy Spirit: *Because you are sons, God sent the Spirit of his Son into our hearts, the Spirit who calls out, "Abba," "Father"* (Gal. 4:6).

The First Three Petitions

As the prayer's initial words serve to address themselves to the god of the covenant, so do the six individual petitions of which it consists. The first three are analogous to the first half of the Ten Commandments in that they are concerned with the cause of God.

The first petition, "Hallowed be thy name," sets as priority number one the glory of God (affirming what is implicit in the third commandment). It is important that our prayer begin here: whatever else we may ask of God, it is presupposed that we desire to take part in the cause of God, which is the glorification of God: the manifestation of his being, goodness, and beauty in creation. Here, as always, Jesus is our model: *It was for this very reason I came to this hour: Father, glorify your name!* (John 12:28)

The second petition, "Thy kingdom come," is a plea for the rule of God to extend into the whole of creation (affirming what is implicit in the fourth commandment [the completion of the divine work, signified by the Sabbath]). The Kingdom of God is the fundamental theme of the scriptures: it is promised in Abraham, it is inaugurated in Moses, it is completed in Christ, and its first harvest in the world is to be found in the Church, but its full harvest will not be complete until the end of all things. The Kingdom of God is wholly present, but not wholly manifest, and will not be so until the sounding of the seventh trumpet, when the saints declare: *The kingdom of the world has now become the kingdom of our Lord and of his Christ, and he will reign forever and ever* (Rev. 11:15).

The third petition, "Thy will be done," is an appeal for the rule of God to extend into the lives of his saints at the present time: because we seek his glory, and because we look to the consummation of his kingdom, we also pray that his will would be done in our lives at the present time (further affirming what is implicit in the fourth commandment [the completion of the divine work, signified by the Sabbath]). A human will perfectly obedient to the divine will is the fullest expression of the Kingdom of God in man: *My Father, if it is possible, may this cup be taken from me. Yet not as I will, but as you will* (Matt. 26:39). And thus, our prayer is that God would be glorified, not only through the advancement of his kingdom, but through the advancement of his kingdom in us: *I have brought you glory on earth by completing the work you gave me to do* (John 17:4).

The Last Three Petitions

The last three petitions are analogous to the second half of the Ten Commandments in that they are concerned with the cause of man. These petitions are bound to the first three petitions inasmuch as the cause of the Creator is expressed in and through his creature, the fullest expression of which is Jesus Christ. As a result, man's requests for himself are neither selfish nor unselfish, for God's will and man's will have become one.

The fourth petition, "Give us this day our daily bread," is a request for the gracious provision of our material, but especially our spiritual needs. Just as the manna in the desert was given on a day-to-day basis, so the present request is not for a surplus but a daily ration, that man may remain conscious of his dependence upon God. This, in turn, draws attention to the fact that man's bread is in the highest sense spiritual: man's spiritual bread is the grace of communion with the divine presence: *I am the bread of life. Your forefathers ate manna in the desert, yet they died. But here is the bread that comes down from heaven, which a man may eat and not die. I am the living bread that came down from heaven. If anyone eats of this bread, he will live forever. This bread is my flesh, which I will give for the life of the world* (John 6:48-51).

The fifth petition, "Forgive us our debts," is a request for the gracious provision of pardon: God not only gives, he for-gives. The giving and the forgiving are related: God gives us the gift of communion, and he forgives us our lack of communion. We are reminded that "sin" refers not only to Adam's act of rebellion against God, but the resultant condition of godlessness in Adam's race. As often as we have cause to pray for the grace of divine communion, so often do we have cause to pray for the grace of forgiveness from sin. When we pray "Forgive us our debts," we should think not only of specific acts of unrighteousness, but of the general condition godlessness out of which such acts emerge: *So I say, love by the Spirit, and you will not gratify the desires of the Sinful Nature. For the Sinful Nature desires what is contrary to the Spirit, and the Spirit what is contrary to the Sinful Nature* (Gal. 5:16-17).

The sixth petition, "Lead us not into temptation, but deliver us from the Evil One" is essentially a request for the provision of an intercessor who can save us from the power of the Evil One. While it is necessary for man to confront evil, it is impossible for fallen man to overcome evil, and therefore we pray for an intercessor to confront evil on our behalf. Jesus Christ is the answer to our prayer: it is he who has been led into temptation on our behalf: *At once the Spirit sent him out into the desert, and he was in the desert forty days being tempted by Satan* (Mark 1:12); and it is he who will continue to be our deliverer: *He has delivered us from such deadly peril, and he will deliver us. On him we have set our hope that he will continue to deliver us...* (II Cor. 1:10). Indeed, the whole of the Lord's Prayer may be understood as a prayer to the Father for the Son: he glorifies the name of the Father, ushers in the Kingdom, performs its commands, fulfills its promises, feeds us with his body, forgives us with his blood, bears the burden of temptation unto death, and delivers us from evil.

CHAPTER THREE

The Light of the Presence

Make the menorah's seven lamps and set them up on it so that they may light the space in front of it.

Exodus 25:37

Prayer is the first step toward the imitation of Christ. It is the imitation of his inner person, whereby we enter into the sanctuary of our souls, and wherein we worship after the pattern set forth in the "Our Father." Again, the purpose of such prayer is our moral sanctification, which is to say the conformation of our will to his will, and this begins above all with the transformation of our ways of thinking: *Do not conform any longer to the pattern of this world, but be transformed by the renewing of your mind* (Rom. 12:2).

Here again, the temple provides an illustration of the acts that are to take place in the inner sanctuary of the soul. As the altar of incense points to the life of continual prayer, so the light of the menorah points to the light of understanding that illumines the mind the one who is joined to the deity in prayer. For God's work of grace consists not only in the gift of his atoning blood, nor only in the gift of his indwelling presence, but also in the gifts that accompany his indwelling presence, and one of these is the gift of light: *For you were chosen that you might declare the praises of him who called you out of darkness and into his wonderful light* (I Pet. 2:9).

In the Bible, God is described as the "Father of Lights. All that mankind perceives or understands is dependent upon him: he is "the true light that gives light to every man" (John 1:9). Moreover, he is the source not only of the general light that shines throughout all of creation (Ps. 19:1-4), but also of the special light that shines through the word of his covenant (Ps. 19:7-11), and which ultimately emanates from the Spirit of Christ (I Pet. 1:11). Accordingly, the one who by prayer regularly invokes the presence of the deity is in effect observing the ancient command to keep the lamps of the sanctuary burning, for he thereby gives continual light to his understanding: *Aaron shall set up the lamps in the Tent of Meeting outside the curtain of the Testimony to burn from evening till morning continually before YHWH—it is a law for all time throughout the ages* (Lev. 24:3).

The Light of Knowledge

By the term "knowledge," I refer to man's theoretical understanding of reality. As mentioned, a common light of reason is given whereby man can discern a whole range of truths, as for example are found in the developed disciplines of philosophy, the humanities, the sciences, mathematics, etc. Moreover, this common light of reason is not condemned to shine upon merely trivial truths, but can at its highest pitch attain to a general revelation of God, inclusive of his existence, his attributes, and his moral laws: *The heavens declare the glory of God, the skies proclaim the work of his hands. Day after day they pour forth speech; night after night they display knowledge. There is no speech or language where their voice is not heart. Their voice goes out into all the earth, their words to the ends of the world* (Psalm 19:1-4).

Furthermore, the fact that reason can attain to a general revelation of God means that it can also stand in a relationship of openness, readiness, and receptivity toward a special revelation of God: that is, a deeper knowledge of God attained via his historic covenant with man (as, for example, we find in the scriptures): *Ask now about the former days, long before your time, from the day God created man on the earth... Has anything so great as this ever happened, or has anything like it ever been heard of? Has any other people heard the voice of God speaking out of fire, as you have, and lived? Has any god ever tried to take for himself one nation out of another nation, by testings, by miraculous signs and wonders, by war, by a mighty hand and an outstretched arm, or by great an awesome deeds, like all the things YHWH your God did for you in Egypt before your very eyes?* (Deut. 4:32-34).

In Jesus Christ, man receives the most comprehensive revelation of God: *He is the image of the invisible God, the firstborn of all creation* (Col. 1:15). He is the light of the world, revealing the fullness of the deity, and therefore the fullness of all that man can know about the deity: *My purpose is that they may have the full riches of complete understanding, in order that they may know the mystery of God, namely Christ, in whom are hidden all the treasures of wisdom and knowledge* (Col. 2:2-3). Such knowledge is foundational to man's spiritual life, for apart from sound theory, he can in no ways have sound practice: *Watch your life and doctrine closely. Persevere in them, because if you do, you will save both yourself and your hearers* (I Tim. 4:16). Such knowledge is cultivated through a life of prayer, where through repeated acts of remembrance its contents are written indelibly on the tablet of the human soul, and through studying the scriptures, the traditions of the church, and the writings of the great theologians—all of whom together constitute the great communion of saints.

On Personal Knowledge of God

Prayer is the first element in man's cultivation of spiritual knowledge. Only in this way does his knowledge acquire a basis in his own personal experience. Among believers today, much of what passes for knowledge amounts to nothing more than what has been handed down by tradition. Of those who embrace this tradition, a few may attempt to appropriate it for themselves on the basis of philosophical or scholarly or scientific inferences. But to verify it directly through the experience of the indwelling Spirit—this is known only to a few.

All of this is simply to suggest what has already been implicit throughout the course of this book: that man is designed to serve as the sanctuary of the deity, and that he is therefore equipped with a spiritual faculty for experiencing God. This spiritual faculty consists in faith, whereby he believes in the god of the covenant, entrusts himself to the terms of that covenant, and enjoys the mediation of his presence in and through the fulfillment of those same terms. It is a spiritual faculty that remains asleep in the life of the unbeliever, but one that has been awakened in the life of the believer. In many cases, however, it is awakened only imperfectly, with the result that a large number of believers are neither wholly asleep nor fully awake, but remain numb to the interior life of the Spirit. It is therefore essential for man's spiritual growth that he be awakened to that kind of faith which knows the deity in lived personal experience: *I know your deeds: you have a reputation of being alive, but you are dead. Wake up* (Rev. 3:1-2)!

The basis of this more experiential kind of knowledge is man's union with the deity. For the man whose life has been joined to that of the deity is not merely a believer, but has by virtue of that belief become a subjective participant in the things of God. His soul has been transformed into a sanctuary of the Holy Spirit: *Do you not know that your body is a temple of the Holy Spirit, who is in you, who you have received from God* (I Cor. 6:19)? As such, he has not merely received testimony about the resurrection, but possesses within himself a positive witness to the resurrection: *The God of our Fathers raised Jesus from the dead... We are witnesses of these things, and so is the Holy Spirit, whom God has given to those who obey him* (Acts 5:30-32). Likewise, he has not merely received testimony about his adoption, but possesses within himself a positive witness to his adoption: *God sent the Spirit of his Son into our hearts, the Spirit who calls out "Abba, Father"* (Gal. 4:6). In other words, these are not merely past events that the believer hears about at secondhand, but present realities that he knows about at firsthand in the form of his own personal experience.

What, then, does it mean to know the deity in personal experience? It means not only to know him by description, but also to know him by acquaintance. A blind man can be taught that the sky is blue (i.e., knowledge by description). But a blind man cannot be taught what it is like to see a blue sky (i.e., knowledge by acquaintance). Likewise, the believer can be taught all of the various attributes of God, but that doesn't mean that he knows what it is like to stand in the presence of the holiness, the righteousness, and the love of God. And yet, this is precisely the kind of knowledge to which the scriptures bear rich poetic witness: "Taste and see that God is good" (Ps. 34:8); "All your robes are fragrant with myrrh and aloes and cassia" (Ps. 45:8); "Today, if you hear his voice, do not harden your hearts" (Ps. 95:7-8). The Psalms in particular give impassioned expression to man's longing for the presence of God: *My heart says of you, "Seek his face!" Your face, YHWH, will I seek. Do not hide your face from me, and do not turn your servant away in anger* (Ps. 27:7-9). Indeed, man's highest aspiration is none other than to dwell in the presence of God: *One thing I ask of YHWH, this is what I seek: that I may dwell in the house of YHWH all the days of my life, to gaze upon the beauty of YHWH and to seek him in his temple* (Ps. 27:4). To be sure, in the present life we are only granted an imperfect vision of the divine presence, but in the life to come we shall behold it in all of its fullness: *Now we see but a poor reflection as in a mirror; then we shall see face to face* (I Cor. 13:12).

On Shared Knowledge of God

But although man's theological knowledge is deeply personal, it is not on that account locked within the narrow domain of his own subjectivity. Rather, it is the common property of the whole community of saints. They are the joint heirs of a shared knowledge, and can therefore speak meaningfully to one another about what they have learned about God through Jesus Christ.

This shared knowledge has been handed down to us in the form of the scripture, the creeds, and the theology of the church. To be sure, they do not all possess the same level of authority, but they nevertheless furnish a map of the spiritual life, consisting of the experiences of thousands of people who have all undertaken this same journey of discipleship. To listen to their voice is to receive light from the Spirit, not as it shines through our own individual life, but as it shines through the collective life of the church: *For we were all baptized by one Spirit into one body—whether Jews or Greeks, slave or free—and we were all given the one Spirit to drink* (I Cor. 12:13).

The basis of this shared knowledge can be found in the fact that the divine presence which indwells the individual is the same as that which has indwelt the whole communion of saints throughout every age of the church: *I have given them the glory that you gave me, that they may be one as we are one: I in them, and you in me* (John 17:22-23). They are all participants in the one life that comes through Jesus Christ, and therefore share in a common experience of fellowship with God, signified in the public ritual of the Lord's Table: *Because there is one loaf, we who are many are one body, for we partake of the one loaf* (I Cor. 10:17). And therefore, it is not just the individual who is a sanctuary, but the whole believing community: *You also, like living stones, are being built into a spiritual house to be a holy priesthood, offering spiritual sacrifices acceptable to God through Jesus Christ* (I Pet. 2:5).

To be sure, this light of shared knowledge is not that of acquaintance, but that of description. To read from Matthew, or from the Apostle's Creed, or from Augustine's "City of God," is not to have experience for oneself, but to encounter the experience of another. And yet this encounter with the other serves to test, expand upon, and contextualize our own experiences, apart from which they very easily fall prey to error, vagueness, and narrow-mindedness. There is always a danger that the individual who has for the first time discovered his faculty for religious experience will begin to think that he is somehow authorized to introduce theological innovations, or escape from intellectual or moral accountability, or indulge in emotional or behavioral extravagance. If, however, the individual does not wax proud and remains humble, the collective witness of the saints should be enough to persuade him that all such imaginings are prompted by human vanity, and not by the Spirit of God. For we are accountable not only to the Spirit that lives within us, but also to the Spirit that lives within the whole Church: *Did the word of God originate with you? Or are you the only people it has reached? If anybody thinks he is a prophet or spiritually gifted, let him acknowledge that what I am writing to you is the Lord's command* (I Cor. 14:36-37).

The Light of Wisdom

Knowledge gives birth to wisdom, which is the light that guides the conduct of man's practical life. The man of wisdom does not live life haphazardly, but he understands the proper end of life, the proper means to attaining that end, and is able to apply what he understands to the particular circumstances of his life through the exercise of discernment.

Here again, we may observe that all men are endowed with a general light of reason whereby they are able to arrive at certain truths of wisdom. Moreover, this natural light of reason is not merely confined to the discovery of trivial truths, but includes within itself profound insights, such as we find in the teachings of both our eastern and western sages. Nevertheless, it remains true that the light that gives light to every man is and remains that of the deity's self-disclosure in his covenant with Israel, so much so that man's native light may be regarded as comparable to darkness.

Thus, the scriptures declare that all true wisdom begins with the knowledge of the Holy One, and specifically that kind of knowledge which is gained through the direct experience of acquaintanceship with him: *The knowledge of the Holy One is understanding, and the fear of YHWH is the beginning of wisdom* (Prov. 9:10). To know YHWH is to encounter one wholly other, and therefore to be humbled by the commonness of one's earthly preoccupations, and to stand in awe before the mystery of his divine purpose: *For my thoughts are not your thoughts, neither are your ways my ways. As the heavens are higher than the earth, so are my ways higher than your ways and my thoughts higher than your thoughts* (Is. 55:8-9). The one who fears him stands receptive to this higher purpose, which finds satisfaction in no creaturely thing, but rather uses creation as a vessel for the manifestation of his divine glory: *He said to me, "You are my servant, Israel, in whom I will display my splendor"* (Is. 49:3).

Knowing the Path

All wisdom begins with the light of remembrance. To forget is to walk in darkness, and the most prevalent cause of spiritual forgetfulness is earthly prosperity: *When you eat and are satisfied, when you build fine houses and settle down, and when your herds and flocks grow large and your silver and gold increase and all you have is multiplied, then your heart will become proud and you will forget YHWH your God* (Deut. 8:12-14).

The wise man remembers what he is: that he belongs to the deity as his earthly sanctuary. In the Old Testament, Job raises what is perhaps the most fundamental question in all of wisdom literature: *What is man that you make so much of him, that you give him so much attention, that you examine him every morning and test him every moment?* (Job 7:17-18). In the New Testament, Paul declares the answer: *Do you not know that your body is a temple of the Holy Spirit? You are not your own; you were bought with a price* (I Cor. 6:19-20).

More than that, however, the wise man remembers what he is for: that the purpose of his life is to bring glory to God, and therefore to manifest his being, his goodness, and his beauty. When an individual forgets this, he begins to live his life according to lesser lights, whether that of mere survival, or that of individual pleasure, achievement, and honor, or that of dedication to whatever he has come to regard as a worthy cause. To be sure, it is a measure of man's nobility whether he dedicates himself to his family, his country, or his race, and in what manner he aims to serve, and to what degree he is willing to sacrifice. But unless his earthly service is set squarely within the service of God, he will be guilty of either consciously or unconsciously worshipping the creature over the Creator: *They worshipped and served created things rather than the Creator—who is forever praised. Amen* (Rom. 1:25). Man is a sanctuary, and therefore his purpose consists in the giving and receiving of glory: *I will see you in the sanctuary, and behold your might and glory. Because your love is better than life, my lips will glorify you* (Ps. 63:2-3).

And finally, the wise man remembers the proper means to this end: that he brings glory to the deity by leading a godly life: *His divine power has given us everything we need for life and godliness through our knowledge of him who called us by his own great glory and goodness* (II Pet. 1:3). To lead a godly life means simply to know him, to enjoy him, and to serve him forever. These three elements may be thought of as steps in a progression: first, we begin to know him; as our knowledge of him increases, we begin to delight in him; and as our delight in him increases, we begin to serve him out of a heart of gladness. This service consists above all in sacrificial works of love, performed among all who claim us as brothers by virtue of our common humanity, and especially among those who claim us as brothers by virtue of our mutual participation in Christ. All of this may sound very high-minded, but it would be a mistake to suppose that the task is too great, or that the secular tasks of life should be set aside in order to devote ourselves to more spiritual tasks. To lead a godly life does not require that we enter into a monastery, but it does require that we allow our souls to be transformed into something very much like a monastery. Our spiritual lives are to consist not only in such acts as prayer along with the natural accompaniments of study, worship, and service, but also in the acts of eating, sleeping, working, playing, caring for ourselves and our families, and looking after the needs of the poor. In a word, spiritual living does not do away with the natural, but purifies it and permeates it with the supernatural, so that all things may be rendered on earth as they are in heaven: *But we have this treasure in jars of clay to show that this all-surpassing power is not from us, but from God* (II Cor. 4:7).

Walking the Path

The path of wisdom can seem very simple when we give expression to it in such clearly formulated counsels. But walking the path is rather a more different matter, since the general principles of which it speaks have to be worked out in the particular context of our own individual life. For while it is true that all believers walk the same path of wisdom, it is equally true that each walks in a manner uniquely his own.

Indeed, one of the first things we discover is that knowing the path does mean that we know how to live it out. Although the principles of our conduct may be formulated in language that is theologically impeccable, the manner in which we apply these principles to our lives can nevertheless become narrow, short-sighted, and even distorted. This, then, calls for the exercise of discernment: the ability to apply what we know generally to our own specific moral situation: *Dear friends, do not believe every spirit, but test the spirits to see whether they are from God* (I John 4:1).

But what does it mean to exercise discernment? How do I distinguish the deity's will from my own will? And how do I avoid the temptation to devise simplistic methods for discerning "the will of God?" To begin with, we should dismiss the notion that recognition of the deity's will takes the form of a mysterious impulse that gives sanction to whatever my current thoughts, feelings, or resolutions happen to be. On the contrary, recognition of the deity's will includes within itself all our natural powers of intellectual, moral, and experiential reasoning, and consists rather in quietly ordering them around the indwelling presence of God. Accordingly, the acquisition of discernment involves the training of our thoughts: *Be transformed by the renewing of your mind* (Rom. 12:3); it involves the training of our affections: *Set your minds on things above, not on earthly things* (Col. 3:2); and it involves the testing of our resolutions in the fires of experience: *Solid food is for the mature, who by constant use have trained themselves to distinguish good from evil* (Heb. 5:14). In short, there is no high road to spiritual discernment: it must be patiently cultivated through a life of prayer and learning and worship and discipleship: *And this is my prayer: that your love may abound more and more in knowledge and depth of insight, so that you may be able to discern what is best...* (Phil. 1:9).

The individual who walks this path of wisdom at last acquires a spiritual history, a living record of what he has experienced in the course of his journey, and this affords a unique source of light that cannot be got from prayer or books or advice. For him, the wisdom of life is not generic but specific, having been planted in the native soil of his own soul. He is therefore not a mere consumer of religious produce, but one who in his own backyard cultivates the things of God, "bringing out of his storeroom new treasures as well as old." This "home-grown" variety of religion is especially important now, when a great many people are engaged in the business of manufacturing and purchasing religious culture, whether in the form of art, music, literature, film, or gala-type events. Indeed, quite a few of our western churches are beginning to look more and more like spiritual marketplaces, their leaders more and more like entrepreneurs, and those who frequent them more and more like shoppers. It hardly needs saying that this approach is devastating for anything that could be called genuine spirituality, for it encourages us to think of spiritual progress in terms of the quantity of what has been consumed by us instead of the quality of what has been ensouled within us. On the contrary, all genuine spirituality consists entirely in the process of "soul-making," so that whatever activities do not result in the deepening of man's consciousness of God or in the ensoulment of godly virtues must be regarded as worldly and unspiritual.

CHAPTER FOUR

The Bread of the Presence

*Put the Bread of the Presence on this table
to be before me at all times.*

Exodus 25:30

I n the Tabernacle, opposite the light of the menorah was a gold table on which was set twelve loaves of bread, eaten by the priests and replaced regularly every week on the Sabbath. Referred to as the "Bread of the Presence," it was the holiest of all the foods the priests enjoyed by virtue of their nearness to the deity, and which they ate on behalf of the twelve tribes whom they represented.

This ritual points to an important truth: that the divine presence is a source not only of light, but also of food. God reveals to man the path of life, and he is at the same time the source of that life. Generally speaking, this is true of all living things that participate in his creation: *YHWH God formed man from the dust of the earth and breathed into his nostrils the breath of life, and the man became a living being* (Gen. 2:7). But it is especially true of those who have become participants in his covenant: *Man does not live on bread alone, but by every word that proceeds from the mouth of YHWH* (Deut. 8:3). YHWH's breath is the spirit that animates the living creature, but his spoken word is the creative power that redeems that spirit from darkness of sin and restores it to the light of holiness.

Thus, YHWH has prepared a table, but man must eat of the food that has been put before him if he is to receive any nourishment from it. This food consists not only in the blood, but especially in the body of Christ, which is above all the earthly vehicle for the gift of his indwelling Spirit: *There is one body and one Spirit* (Eph. 4:4). And thus, to eat of the bread that came down from heaven means by faith to receive the gift of the divine presence, and by faith to abide in the midst of this divine presence: *Remain in me, and I will remain in you* (John 15:4). By abiding in the presence of God, we grow in the depth of our acquaintanceship with him, and thereby condition our hearts to an affective love of him, which is a necessary prelude to any service that comes from a genuine spirit of thanksgiving.

The Cultivation of Holiness

Jesus Christ is the temple of the living God. Through the washing of his blood, and through the gift of his incarnate spirit, the life of the believer has also been transformed into a temple. It is therefore both his duty as well as his privilege to behold the glory of the Father, through the mediation of the Son, and in the power of the indwelling Holy Spirit: *Father, I want those you have given me to be with me where I am, and to see my glory, the glory you have given me because you loved me before the creation of the world* (John 17:24).

By faith we receive his presence, and by that same faith we remain attentive to his presence in the midst of our earthly lives. Faith, therefore, is not merely a matter of belief, nor simply one of trust, but one of intuition. Although this may seem difficult at first, by faithfully practicing the presence of God, we gradually become accustomed to beholding it for longer periods of time and at greater levels of depth. And ultimately, it is through this inner discipline of beholding the divine glory that the spiritual faculties of our soul are awakened to a sensitive, appetitive, and affectionate love for God: *You will fill me with joy in your presence, with eternal pleasures at your right hand* (Ps. 16:11).

The practical upshot is simply this: that, in opposition to our native inclination toward sin, there is implanted in us a contrary inclination toward the holiness of God. For the one who eats of the bread of heaven will find that it has the peculiar quality of both satisfying and creating a hunger for more. This holy hunger is as fire for the purification of our souls, contending with all that is sinful and drawing the heart more deeply into the mystery of holiness, so that the affections of the heart may at last come to rest upon their proper object, the greatest of all possible beings: *Blessed are the pure in heart, for they will see God* (Matt. 5:8).

The Meditative Experience of God

Although the world intrudes upon our senses whether we will it to or not, the deity only comes to those who earnestly seek him. In other words, if we are content to live our lives without taking time out to meditate, it should not surprise us that we can point to no definite experience of God. Again, to meditate is to listen to God as he speaks his word through creation, through his covenant, and through the gift of his indwelling presence. By meditating on his word at length, we are able not only to imprint it on the tablet of our souls, but to appropriate it as a word spoken to us individually, whereby it may begin to evoke those religious sensitivities, appetites, and affections in which alone we can claim to have personal knowledge of God.

The most fundamental attribute of the deity revealed in his covenant is that of his divine holiness. Indeed, in the very act of revelation he is disclosed as one who transcends the created order because he enters it so to speak from the outside. He is the wholly other, the one whose being, goodness, and beauty lie beyond the reach of man's natural comprehension, and who man is forbidden to identify with any of the familiar powers of the world. Nevertheless, all this simply amounts to knowledge by description unless we are able to enter into the presence of the deity and experience it for ourselves in the form of fear and humility. Fear and humility are the bedrock of the believer's religious affections, the soil out of which all of his other religious feelings grow. This remains true even after he has been forgiven and accepted by God, for as long as the deity remains holy and he remains a sinner, the awful fact of his alienation will always accompany the joyous fact of his reconciliation. It is crucial therefore to cultivate an interior atmosphere of soul in which both of these sensitivities flourish: a profound awe toward God, and an equally profound humility toward oneself: *But I, by your great mercy, will come into your house; and in thy fear I will worship toward your holy temple* (Ps. 5:7)

After the deity's holiness, we come to his righteousness. Here, I refer not to his justice as measured by human standards, but to his justice as measured by the eternal standard of his own holiness. This is to be found in the faithfulness he exhibits to the terms of his covenant, in which he has pronounced the sentence of death upon every kind of evil and in which he has bestowed the reward of life upon all "who by persistence in doing good seek glory, honor, and immortality" (Rom. 2:7). In Jesus Christ, the terms of this covenant are fulfilled, and therefore the righteousness of the deity is vindicated. But again, while such knowledge by description is valuable, it is intended to become ensouled within us by a feeling of reverence for his righteousness and by a feeling of contrition over our unrighteousness. By reverence, I mean a feeling of deep respect for the moral greatness of God, and by contrition I mean a feeling of sorrow as well as hunger to amend the moral failure that is so prevalent in our lives: *Revere him, all you descendants of Israel! For he has not despised or disdained the suffering of the afflicted one; he has not hidden his face from him but has listened to his cry for help… Posterity will serve him; future generations will be told about YHWH. They will proclaim his righteousness to a people yet unborn—for he has done it* (Ps. 22:23-31).

Finally, the meditation of our hearts should come to rest upon the love of God. Again, however, this is not to be sought in any popular conception of love, as if his love arose out of a longing for fellowship with us or out of a desire to help us get along in the world. On the contrary, his love for us arises out of the fact that he is in his divine nature infinitely charitable, and that he is therefore eternally resolved to fit us for the supreme gift of his holiness. His covenant, therefore, is not only an expression of his righteousness, but also of his love, through which he offers the gift of forgiveness and the gift of his divine presence. And herein lies the richest source of our religious affections, for it is out of forgiveness that we have peace, and it is in the deity's presence that we have joy, and it is through both that we find the gratitude and affection which alone can move us to the heartfelt expression of thanksgiving and praise. All of these religious affections mark progressive stages in the unfolding of man's love for God. As his affective love increases, in such measure does his capacity for effective love increase, culminating in a life of obedience to the commandments of God. And thus, it is through joy that he is initiated into a life of service: *Shout for joy to YHWH, all the earth! Enter his gates with thanksgiving and his courts with praise; give thanks to him and praise his name. For YHWH is good and his love endures forever* (Ps. 100:1-5).

The Contemplative Experience of God

In contemplative prayer, we direct our attention to the divine presence, but without meditating upon any specific element of the deity's person or work. Rather, our focus rests solely on the fact that he is present with us in all places and at all times and in the midst of all the more mundane affairs of our earthly existence. He is present when I awake, when I eat my breakfast, when I go to work, when I clean my house, when I think, when I read, when I watch television, when I talk, when I argue. Thus, the Psalmist declares: *I am always mindful of the presence of YHWH* (Ps. 16:8).

When the eye of the mind is fixed upon the deity's presence, all the richness of who he is and what he has done is communicated to us within the mystery of his divine simplicity. To be sure, when we think at length about him, his being appears to us as something infinitely complex; but when we set our minds at rest in the knowledge of his presence, his being appears in the truest light of its infinite simplicity. His presence contains within itself the fullness of his divine glory, of his being, goodness, and beauty, and of all that has been and will ever be accomplished through the mediation of his historic covenant. He is the "I Am," the one whose being is identical with his essence, and whose name is therefore ineffable: *I saw heaven standing open and there before me was a rider on a white horse... He has a name written on him that no one knows but he himself* (Rev. 19:11-12).

Because such prayer has its basis in the divine simplicity, the way in which we experience it is correspondingly simple. His presence is not encompassed within the narrow domain of any finite feeling, but is experienced as an all-encompassing sense of rest, completeness, *shalom*. The totality of all that man has experienced or is capable of experiencing, from his sense of awe and fear, to his feelings of reverence and contrition and hunger for righteousness, to his feelings of peace, joy, gratitude, affection, thanks, and praise—everything is captured within the simplicity of finding rest in the one who has established his rest in us. Thus, God exhorts his people: *Be still and know that I am God* (Ps. 46:10). And the Psalmist says of himself: *My heart is not proud, YHWH. I do not concern myself with great matters or things too wonderful for me. But I have stilled and quieted my soul; like a weaned child with its mother, like a weaned child is my soul within me* (Ps. 131:1-2).

To some, the kind of mystical experience I am describing might appear to be devoid of any real content. But while it is true that some silences arise out of a lack of content, it also true that some silences arise out of a superabundance of content. Indeed, we all know from ordinary experience that the more two people have come to know one another, the less chatter is required in order for them to communicate. The same holds true here, for which reason it should not be regarded as a substitute, but rather as an extension of the disciplines of study, verbal prayer, and meditation. It is a way of allowing that which has become ensouled within us to permeate our lives in all places, at all times, and in the midst of every activity. For this reason, it has sometimes been referred to as "acquired contemplation," indicating that our intuition of the deity's presence does not consist in setting aside what we have understood or experienced, but rather in binding all of it together in the mystery of his being. This can be seen in the fact that a presentiment of all these things is often found to accompany the more simple apprehension of his presence. What is most important, however, is that in beholding him we are continually aware of the fact that he beholds us, and that the fullness of all we could ever say or do is eternally disclosed to him: *O YHWH, you have searched me and you know me. You know when I sit and when I rise; you perceive my thoughts from afar. You discern my going out and my lying down; you are familiar with all my ways. Before a word is on my tongue, you know it completely, O YHWH* (Ps. 139:1-4).

The Mortification of Sin

If holiness is about feeding on the presence of God, then the mortification of sin is about learning to abstain from those things that are not real food. To mortify sin means to put it to death, or rather to allow it to be put to death by the operation of the Spirit: *For if you live according to the flesh you will die, but if by the Spirit you mortify the deeds of the flesh you will live* (Rom. 8:13).

As we have seen in the previous section, the cultivation of holiness is like the kindling of a flame, for it manifests itself in a desire to consume everything that is contrary to itself. And thus, even though the mortification of sin amounts to a kind of purgatory for the soul, it is nevertheless a joyful undertaking, for it consists in the free satisfaction of a holy hunger. By contrast, a heart that has no share in this holy hunger will find it difficult to make progress along the road to mortification, for how can it deny itself earthly joys unless it does so in the pursuit of one supreme heavenly joy? It is in spiritual hunger and in the joy of its satisfaction that we discover the power of the indwelling Spirit: *The joy of YHWH is your strength* (Neh. 8:10).

Thus, the goal of mortification is not to make ourselves worthy to enter the deity's presence, for this has already been accomplished in the sacrificial work of Jesus Christ. Rather, it presupposes that we are already at peace with God, and therefore consists in making our joy complete by bringing us into greater fellowship with the life of the Triune God. Nevertheless, it would be naive to assume that because the journey begins with joy that it does not also entail suffering. On the contrary, the more single-mindedly we pursue the object of our joy, the more likely it is that the pursuit will cause us suffering. For the sinful nature is no abstract idea, but is woven into the psychological tissue of our soul, and recoils as much as any living thing at the prospect of its crucifixion. It does not care to have its motives examined, still less to have them denied, and is not likely to go along quietly with head bowed to the place of execution. We must be realistic therefore, accepting that the joyful pursuit of holiness will bring with it a proportionate measure of earthly suffering: *Let us fix our eyes on Jesus, the author and perfecter of our faith, who for the joy set before him endured the cross, scorning its shame, and sat down at the right hand of the throne of God* (Heb. 12:2-3).

The Practice of Self-Examination

Sin thrives on anonymity. The passions prefer nothing more than to go to work every day without having to hear the sound of their own names. Therefore, the first step in the process of mortification is to shine the light of the deity's presence into every corner of the soul in order that we might know what is living inside of us and what it is up to: *Search me, O God, and know my heart; test me and know my anxious thoughts. See if there is any offensive way in me, and lead me in the way everlasting* (Ps. 139:23-24).

Naturally, what we find when we shine the light of the deity into our soul will be quite specific. And yet, we are not on that account unable to speak about it generally, for as there is only one standard of holiness, so there is no sin that has taken hold of us that is not common to all mankind. In the broadest possible sense, sin can be described as a condition of godlessness: to say that we are sinners is to say we are vacated temples, overrun by a legion of disordered thoughts, feelings, and behaviors. The heart, in the absence of its native infinite object, has become absorbed in itself, in others, and in a multiplicity of finite things, so that what might otherwise have been a garden of natural loves has instead become a wilderness of unnatural cravings. At its heart, sin consists in the distortion, disordering, and perversion of love: *They exchanged the truth of God for a lie, and worshipped and served created things rather than the Creator. Because of this, God gave them over to shameful lusts* (Rom. 1:25-26).

As for the more particular forms of sin, there are seven according to the classical enumeration, though the specific ones mentioned vary from list to list. In the following discussion, I limit myself to three because they appear to include in their scope all of the others: pride, anger, and lust. At the head of the list is pride, the greatest of the vices, and the opposite of godly fear and humility. To be proud is to esteem oneself over all others, and to secure this esteem for oneself by attempting to be more, do more, or have more than the next person. For this reason, it seeks above all else the power to control, the ability to bend people and circumstances into conformity with our own will. And yet, its deadliness does not consist simply in the fact that it is a cause of great social evils, but especially in the fact that it bars us from the fulfillment of our destiny, which is to know, enjoy, and serve God. If, however, pride may be regarded as sin's root, anger and lust may be regarded as its two primary branches. Anger is very near to pride, since the inordinate irritation that characterizes it arises out of the frustration of our will, and therefore reveals that our hearts are not content to rest in God's will. And lust is very near to pride, since the inordinate desire that characterizes it arises out of our preoccupation with such earthly goods as luxury, food, and sex, and therefore reveals that our hearts harbor a secret preference for the world over God. In both cases, the pleasure that results from ventilating anger or indulging desire tempts us to disobey the commands of God, and to behave in a manner unworthy of our divine calling.

Once the nature of sin has been recognized in general, and once its forms have been acknowledged in particular, then the real process of mortification begins. But just as the cultivation of holiness involves a lengthy process of "en-souling," so the mortification of sin involves a lengthy process of "de-souling." It is a process of change that moves from the inside out: beginning with our thoughts, passing to our feelings, and only in the final stage affecting our behavior. As for our thought-life, we must begin by trying to see sin for what it really is, for unless our heads are able to grasp the rationale behind the commandments, it is foolish to suppose that our hearts will ever begin to sympathize with them, and still more foolish to suppose that our hands will be empowered to keep them. And the first point is this, that sin is a condition before it is an act: it is because of the godlessness of our minds that we perform godless acts. In other words, our greatest sin is one of omission rather than one of commission, for we habitually neglect the first of the commandments, which is that of attentive love toward God and that of attentive love toward God's children. Until we are able to grasp sin at this most fundamental level, we will never be able to recover that unshakeable conviction that lies at the heart of all genuine spiritual seeking: that I am a sinner. Moreover, it is here that we learn the rational behind the aforementioned sins of commission, for all of them in the final analysis are born out of the fact that we have love for neither God nor our neighbor. Pride prioritizes my self over all other selves;

anger prioritizes my will over all other wills; and lust prioritizes my desires over any other values that might exercise a restraining influence upon them. This, then, is the truth about sin which we are to understand, and on account of which we ought to be repulsed: that it despises God, and that it degrades the human soul which is meant to serve his temple.

The Practice of Self-Denial

If sin is godlessness, then our primary method of dealing with it does not consist in trying to pre-empt the first beginnings of sin, but rather in the cultivation of holiness. To direct all of our attention to the task of pre-empting future actions is to inadvertently suppose that there is nothing wrong with us in the meantime. But as we have already seen, our inattentiveness to the deity is precisely the problem, whereas specific sinful acts are but a symptom of this problem. Mortification, then, begins in the here and now: it sets aside the fruitless worry about what we may or may not do in the future, and gives all of its attention to the emptiness and corruption of our hearts in the present. It poses two questions: What desires at present are competing with my devotedness to God? And how can I deny them those provisions to which they appear to have a lawful claim, but which are inevitably revealed as a snare when they demand them against all lawful restraint?

We should be clear: all mortification involves self-denial, but not in an unqualified sense. We deny ourselves not because there is some inherent virtue in self-denial, but in order that our earthly appetites may be bridled and placed in the service of a supreme heavenly appetite. Here again, we are reminded that the pursuit of holiness will always be accompanied by a proportionate measure of suffering in our sinful nature. As the runner knows that his labor will be accompanied by pain, so the one who undertakes to mortify his sin may expect his flesh to recoil. But again, just as the runner's passion to reach the finish line enables him to endure the pain of fatigue, so the believer's passion for holiness enables him to endure the pain of self-denial. It is through spirit-inspired passion that the work of mortification is made possible: *Clothe yourselves with the Lord Jesus Christ, and make no provision for the flesh, to gratify its desires* (Rom. 13:14).

The practice of self-denial is in the first place mental. It is man's acquired habit to neglect his spiritual growth, and to indulge in an aimless stream of rambling thoughts, facilitated either by his own imagination or by the press, the radio, or the television. All of this naturally crowds out any chance of his practicing the presence of God, and the more accustomed he is to such outside stimulants the more violently his flesh resists any suggestion of a change in lifestyle. But if he is truly serious about growing in holiness and mortifying sin, he is going to have to submit himself to what can only be described as a kind of mental fast. At the same time, he must remember that such mental fasting is in vain if it does not issue forth in his learning how to feed upon Christ. It is indeed necessary for every believer to enter into this dark night of the soul, but this is only in order that they might be trained to behold more clearly the light of the supernatural God: *Set your minds on things above, not on earthly things* (Col. 3:2).

Mental self-denial leads to physical self-denial. If we are willing to deny ourselves earthly imaginings, then we should also be willing to deny ourselves earthly pleasures. Again, we are not here speaking about abstaining from things unlawful, but about abstaining from things lawful, such as rest, food, and sexual activity. Accordingly, the purpose of doing this is not in order to avoid sin, but in order to train the soul to say no to earthly passions and to increase its stamina for a more extended pursuit of spiritual things. It is to subject the soul to the same kind of disciplined exercise with which we train the body for health, athletics, and war. For, if we are unpracticed in doing these things when the stakes are low, it is rather foolish to suppose that we shall have success in doing them when the stakes are high. Therefore Paul declares: *I beat my body and make it my slave, so that after I have preached to others, I will not myself be disqualified for the prize* (I Cor. 9:27).

CHAPTER FIVE

The Kingdom of Prophets and Priests

To him who loves us and has freed us from our sins by his blood,
and has made us to be a kingdom and priests to serve his God
and Father—to him be glory and power forever and ever!

Revelation 1:5-6

In chapter one, we began with the idea of the Kingdom of God. God is the great king over creation, and his governance over his creatures, suppressed in the fall but restored in his covenant, culminates in the establishing of his sanctuary. Like Moses before him, Jesus leads his people out of the bondage of sin, carrying them through the waters of baptism, and bringing them to a law and a temple that he established in their hearts through the gift of his blood and the impartation of his Spirit.

But as with the nation of Israel, a final task remains: to go up and take possession of the land. All authority in heaven and on earth has been given to Christ (Matt. 28:18-20), and by virtue of that authority he has made the community of believers the inheritors of the earth (Matt. 5:5). It is therefore the task of believers not only to realize the governance of the deity within their own souls, but to realize the governance of the deity within the souls of all men, so that the quality of holiness might permeate the whole of creation: *They will neither harm nor destroy on all my holy mountain, for the earth will be filled with the knowledge of the glory of YHWH, as the waters cover the sea* (Is. 11:9).

It is for this reason that we speak of a kingdom of prophets and priests, for it is through the administration of these offices that the deity's governance advances throughout the world. It is not a conquest of men's bodies through the power of the sword, but a conquest of men's souls through the power of truth and grace. And therefore it is not only the soul of the individual that is a temple (I Cor. 6:19), but it is the souls of all believers everywhere throughout the ages that together constitute one vast cosmic temple (I Pet. 2:5). As their numbers increase, the building of this temple draws near the day of its completion, a day on which not only the souls of the dead will be raised, but on which the created order itself will be resurrected: *Then I saw a new heaven and a new earth, for the first heaven and the first earth had passed away, and there was no longer any sea* (Rev. 21:1). And herein lies the hope of the believer, to come to the new heaven and the new earth, and to rest in the beatific vision of the face of God: *Now we see but a poor reflection as in a mirror; then we shall see face to face. Now I know in part; then I shall know fully, even as I am fully known* (I Cor. 13:12).

The Prophetic Administration of Truth

At the popular level, a prophet is regarded as one whose business is to predict the future. But while it is true that the biblical prophets spoke of future events, this was only a small part of their ministry, which consisted rather in proclaiming the Word of the Lord.

In the earliest stages of biblical history, the prophets were referred to as "seers" (I Sam. 9:9). This apparently obscure fact points to an important truth, for whereas it was the business of the scribes to give an account of what had been handed down to them, it was the business of the prophets to give an account of what they had themselves seen. In other words, the prophets were the firsthand witnesses of the truth, men who had stood in the presence of the deity, and who were therefore in a position to speak with the voice of authority. Moreover, while this prophetic office was initially held by only a few, it was ultimately intended for all members of the covenant, who through the outpouring of the Spirit would be brought into direct union with God: *And afterward, I will pour out my Spirit on all flesh; your sons and daughters shall prophesy; your old men shall dream dreams, and your young men shall see visions* (Joel 2:28).

As for the content of the prophetic word, it culminates in Jesus Christ: *The testimony of Jesus is the spirit of prophecy* (Rev. 19:10). In other words, all prophetic speech may be said to consist in the unfolding of what has already been handed down in the message of the gospel: *But when the Spirit of truth comes, he will guide you into all truth. He will not speak on his own, he will speak only what he hears, and he will tell you what is yet to come. He will bring glory to me by taking from what is mine and making it known to you* (John 16:13-14). For this reason, everyone who believes in the gospel may be said to have virtual access to the full content of prophetic utterance, in which one individual differs from another only in degree of calling, insight, and experience: *Follow the way of love and eagerly desire spiritual gifts, especially the gift of prophecy... For everyone who prophesies speaks to men for their strengthening, encouragement, and comfort... He who prophesies edifies the church* (I Cor. 14:1-4).

The Prophetic Word

As the foregoing passage indicates, the prophet's first duty is to speak the word of truth among his fellow believers. This means that a large part of his prophetic office is discharged simply in teaching, exhorting, and encouraging the body of believers. Furthermore, while this is a task that the church leadership can be expected to hold in pre-eminence, it also a task to which each individual believer is called within their own individual sphere of influence: *Let the word of Christ dwell in your richly as you teach and admonish one another with all wisdom, and as you sing psalms, hymns, and spiritual songs with gratitude in your hearts to God* (Col. 3:16).

At the same time, prophetic ministry is not merely confined to the church, but extends to those outside the community of believers. In Jesus' Parable of the Sower, he says that the deity's kingdom is intended to advance throughout the whole earth, and that it is like a farmer planting a seed in the ground. In the interpretation of this parable which he later gives to his disciples, the seed is identified with the gospel, and therefore with the power of new life. For this reason, Paul makes it clear that the most important part of evangelization is not the visible work done by the one who plants, but the invisible work done by the seed itself: *Neither he who plants nor he who waters is anything, but only God, who makes things grow* (I Cor. 3:7).

Nevertheless, the one who sows also has an important role to play. True, he does not possess in himself anything that could be added to the gospel, but his words may certainly do more or less justice to the gospel, and to that extent they can act as either a help or a hindrance. Therefore, Paul says: *Pray for us, that God may open a door for our message, and that we may proclaim the mystery of Christ. Pray that I may proclaim it clearly, as I should* (Col. 4:3-4). The fact that he regarded his work as a messenger to be an important element in the advance of the gospel can be seen above all in how much time he devotes in his letters to discussing his own qualifications as an apostle: e.g., the authenticity of his conversion, his divine commission, his personal motives, his work ethic, etc. Nevertheless, his most important qualification always remains his faithfulness to the word that has been handed down to him: *Now it is required that those who have been given a trust must prove faithful. I care very little if I am judged by you or by any human court; indeed, I do not even judge myself... It is the Lord who judges me* (I Cor. 4:2-4).

As a final observation, we may also note that the power of

the gospel can be helped or hindered by the kind of soil in which it is sown. Accordingly, the Parable of the Sower describes three different kinds of soil in which the seed of the gospel cannot thrive: (1) soil that is found on the broad path of life; (2) soil that is of shallow depth; (3) and soil that is choked with weeds. In short, there are conditions in the human heart that can render it unreceptive, barren, or inimical to the word of truth. When it comes to truth's ability to succeed in the world, therefore, the fault never lies with the seed, and while on occasion it may lie with the sower, it most frequently lies with the kind of soil in which it is sown. A heart that is hard, or shallow, or entangled in earthly things has fortified itself against the truth, and while such a heart is not beyond remedy, it cannot be healed against its will: *When Jesus saw the man lying there and learned that he had been in this condition for a long time, he asked him, "Do you want to get well?"* (John 5:6). This means that an individual's journey toward faith begins far in advance of his actually hearing the gospel, for the ruin of his soul and the hope of redemption remain invisible, silent, and persistent witnesses that continually beckon him heavenward. Evangelism can provide an external aid for the direction of this inner voice, but in the end it can never be anything more than an aid: *God will give to each person according to what he has done. To those who by persistence in doing good seek glory, honor, and immortality, he will give eternal life. But for those who are self-seeking and who reject the truth and follow evil, there will be wrath and anger* (Rom. 2:6-8).

The Prophetic Life

In the Bible, the prophets gave expression to the truth not only by their words, but more importantly through their lives. They were not merely mouthpieces for divine revelation, but flesh-and-blood individuals who had been deeply moved by an encounter with God. Accordingly, the divine word achieved expression not only in what they said, but in how they said it, and how it affected their life. And this must be equally true of the life of every genuine believer, that he does not merely speak, but that he is a direct participant in that of which he speaks, and therefore that the whole of his life comes to reverberate with the Word of God.

Thus, the prophetic life begins with that faith through which man encounters the living God. Such an encounter does not merely consist in the hearing of words, but in a heightened awareness of the deity's presence, accompanied by deep moral conviction, and with much fear and trembling. It is not like other earthly experiences, which come to us through our outward senses. It is rather what the scriptures describe as a "still small voice," spoken into the quiet interiority of our soul (I Kgs. 19:11-13). As such, its authenticity is not measured by its outward intensity, but by its ability to produce inward certainty, for this is the hallmark of the prophet—that he is one who has seen for himself: *For we know, brothers loved by God, that he has chosen you, because our gospel came to you not simply with words, but also with power, with the Holy Spirit, and with deep conviction* (I Thess. 1:4-5).

At the same time, the prophet is not only one who has seen God, but also one who has the heart of God. He is not only ritually holy, but he is morally holy, meaning that the quality of godliness has been en-souled within him, so that his heart inclines after the things of God. More than anything else, it is this acquired passion for holiness that accounts for the verbal and behavioral extravagance of the biblical prophets. The prophets don't speak, they boil over: praising all that is of God, ranting against all that is ungodly, castigating the rich, crying out on behalf of the poor, and proclaiming the imminent day of judgment. If we are prepared to dismiss such heightened spiritual sensitivity as a kind of hysteria, shall we then condone the callous indifference to evil that now passes for normal? Then, as now, the heart is intended to serve as an instrument of the divine pathos: *YHWH will seek out a man after his own heart* (I Sam. 13:14).

Finally, the prophetic life is marked by the fact that it willingly endures suffering in the service of God. An individual possessed of an infinite good has a corresponding capacity to persevere under finite suffering. In turn, this testifies to his authenticity as a messenger, for no one suffers for a thing unless he believes in it. In addition, it testifies to the glory of his message, for we often measure the value of a thing with reference to how much someone is willing to suffer for it. It is in this sense that we can speak of the cross as a revelation of the glory of the Father: *Let us fix our eyes on Jesus, who for the joy set before him endured the cross...* (Heb. 12:2). It is in this sense that we must also understand the suffering of the apostles: *This man is my chosen instrument to carry my name before the Gentiles and the people of Israel. I will show him how much he must suffer for my name* (Acts 9:15-16). And it is in this sense that we must understand our own sufferings whenever they are endured on behalf of the gospel: *For it has been granted to you on behalf of Christ not only to believe on him, but also to suffer for him* (Phil. 1:29).

The Priestly Administration of Grace

The prophetic word declares man's sin and the deity's holiness, and this can be seen as setting the agenda for the work of the priesthood. The priest serves as a mediator between the domains of sin and holiness, a task made possible through the intervention of grace.

Gratia means essentially "gift." As such, grace is not given out of need or expectation of return, but out of the generosity of the giver. For this reason, the exchange of grace among friends is quite natural, whereas the giving of grace to an enemy brings with it painful sacrifice. Moreover, in the case of man's relation to God, the giving of grace is not simply in order to right certain wrongs, but in order to restore man to his original state. And thus, divine grace consists not only in the gift of forgiveness, but also in the gift of the divine presence, whereby the soul of man is brought back into its proper condition of dependence upon God.

In the new sanctuary of the soul, the priesthood of believers discharges the duties of their office through acts of forgiveness and charity. As by faith they have received pardon and life, so out of the abundance of what they have received they are obligated to extend pardon and life to others. Nevertheless, it is clear that these fruits of love do not come about through any power of their own, and so their ability to produce them will largely be determined by the extent to which their souls are actually participating in the reality of grace. This in turn calls for self-examination: it is very easy to pay lip service to spiritual realities to which our mind gives no great attention. Humanly speaking, it is certainly understandable if we find it difficult to give or forgive, but we must nevertheless concede that such difficulties are often a sign of spiritual poverty.

On Forgiving

The Christian is obliged to forgive. He forgives because he has been forgiven. And by the same token, if he refuses to forgive others, he forgoes the forgiveness that is offered to him: *For if you forgive men when they sin against you, your heavenly Father will also forgive you. But if you do not forgive men their sins, your heavenly Father will not forgive your sins* (Matt. 6:14-15).

The obligation to forgive is often misunderstood. To forgive a person who has wronged me does not mean that I have to feel affectionate toward them, nor does it means that I have to condone their behavior, nor does it mean that I have to protect them from the consequences of their behavior. It does, however, mean that I have to renounce my anger, my resentment, and my desire for personal restitution. In other words, the one who forgives has not been deprived of his rights, but has freely laid them down in order that he might devote himself more fully to the welfare of his neighbor: *Bear with each other and forgive whatever grievances you may have against one another. And over all these virtues put on love, which binds them all together in perfect unity* (Col. 3:13-14).

Because this obligation to forgive arises out of our relationship with God, it follows that the power to forgive does not lie within our own nature as such. If we are to forgive, then, we must cease to look at our lives from our own vantage point, and we must strive to see ourselves and others from the vantage point of God. We ought to be mindful of our own wretchedness, and we ought to be mindful of the fact that those who we call our enemies are loved by God. Only in this way will we be able to diffuse our indignation and learn to pray for the well-being of those who oppress us: *You have heard that it was said, "Love your neighbor and hate your enemy." But I tell you: Love your enemies and pray for those who persecute you, that you may be sons of your Father in heaven* (Matt. 5:43-45).

The task of forgiveness is uniquely challenging. In some cases, the challenge comes from the gravity of the offense. In other cases, the challenge comes from the repetitious nature of the offense, since this calls for repeated acts of forgiveness. In relationships, for example, it is not uncommon for an unwarranted expectation of forgiveness to be countered by a refusal to forgive, especially when there has been a history of repeated offenses. There is a very natural fear that the inexhaustibility of forgiveness will render it a cloak for the perpetuation of injustice. Again, however, the obligation to forgive does not mean that one has to enjoy, condone, or set aside appropriate consequences for destructive behavior. It does mean that we must replace hatred with love, and that we must be prepared to do so on a regular basis: *Peter came to Jesus and asked, "Lord, how many times shall I forgive my brother when he sins against me? Up to seven times?" Jesus answered, "I tell you, not seven times, but seventy times seven"* (Matt. 18:21-22).

On Giving

All Christian love expresses itself in charity, which may be broadly defined as the act of giving. Love, as manifested in the act of giving, is the highest expression of spiritual life, of moral holiness, and of the imitation of Christ. The more we are able to give, the more we testify to the abundance of the spirit living within us, whose glory is manifested in the ability to give sacrificially—even to the point of death.

Unfortunately, charity is often thought of in very superficial ways, as though it consisted simply in being nice, or in making occasional monetary donations, or in going on missions trips. While such individual acts are not devoid of value, the real business of charity consists in the performance of repeated acts over a lengthy period of time in the context of committed relationships. In other words, charity is vocational: it is not so much an act in which one gives away things as much as it is an occupation in which one is regularly called upon to give of oneself. Here, a general calling goes forth to all men to seek committed relationships within the institutions of work, family, society, and church. These are not simply individual initiatives of our own, but they are divine mandates through which our lives are bound to the lives of others into an organic whole. If we do not bind ourselves in any of these ways, or if we are in the habit of repeatedly making and breaking such covenants, we may still have the opportunity to perform various charitable acts, but we will never learn in a deeper sense what it means to live a charitable life.

By answering the call to charity vocationally, by giving ourselves to the divine mandates of work, family, society, and church, we enter into a concrete life-situation in which we no longer have the luxury of holding others at arm's length. These are not glorious undertakings, but humble forms of service, bringing with them a host of mundane practical problems. Indeed, one of our first discoveries will be the depth to which human relationships have been corrupted by sin, and the deep spiritual resources that are required to sustain charity in the face of the system of buying and selling upon which so much of our fallen world depends. For example, if we are to be charitable in our work, then we must cease to think of it simply as a way of making money, and strive to realize in it a genuine service to our families, our communities, and our churches. Again, marriage should not be thought of simply as a means to personal fulfillment, but as a vehicle through which men and women cooperate in the raising of children, and through which they perpetuate the family as the fundamental unit of human life. Likewise, the institutions of the government and the church do not exist merely in order to serve us, but in order that we might have an opportunity to serve the larger interests of humanity and the people of God.

As is clear in the foregoing, all of these relationships have the potential to cause us suffering. Such suffering can come in the form of disappointment, or failure, or pain caused by the people or circumstances to which we are bound. In all of these cases, however, the real test of charity is found in its ability to persevere in the face of suffering. In other words, we must persist in being charitable, not only in the face of our own displeasure, but even in the face of insult and injury. YHWH's commitment to Israel provides the supreme example of this, a commitment he maintained in spite of her repeated failure and hostility, and which climaxed in the suffering and death of Jesus Christ. Jesus' teaching made it clear, however, that he was by no means a passive victim of other people's aggression. On the contrary, he freely chose to take up the cross, for it was his firm resolution to remain committed to his people regardless of how they treated him: *I am the good shepherd. The good shepherd lays down his life for the sheep... No one takes it from me, but I lay it down of my own accord* (John 10:11-18). Therefore, Christians are commanded to imitate the pattern of returning good for evil, and to measure their own sufferings by the pattern set down by Christ: *Consider him who endured such opposition from sinful men, so that you will not grow weary and lose heart. In your struggle against sin, you have not yet resisted to the point of shedding your blood* (Heb. 12:3-4).

CPSIA information can be obtained at www.ICGtesting.com
Printed in the USA
BVOW071058230413

318896BV00001B/3/P